To Soshant Bali,
putting down roots in 21st-century California

CONTENTS

MICHIGAN

Lake Erie

PENNSYLVANIA

INDIANA

FAIRFIELD

WEST VIRGINIA

KENTUCKY

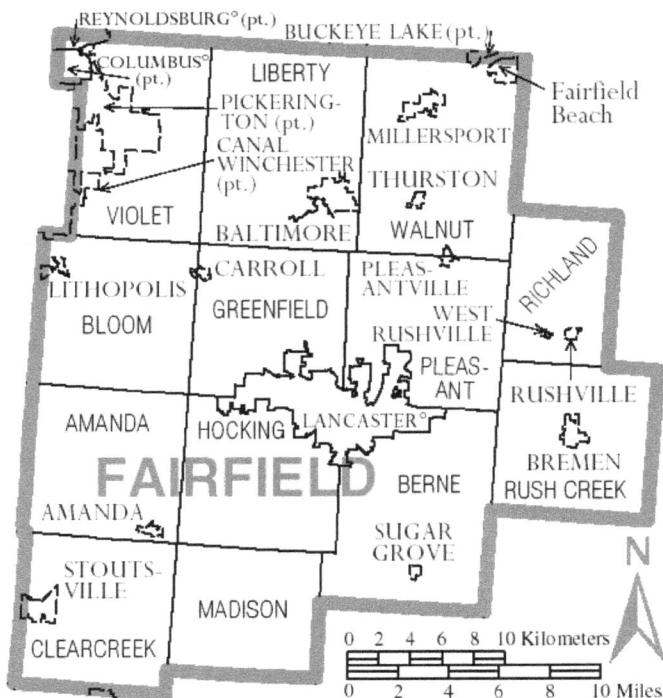

REYNOLDSBURG° (pt.)
BUCKEYE LAKE (pt.)
COLUMBUS° (pt.)
LIBERTY
Fairfield Beach
PICKERINGTON (pt.)
MILLERSPORT
CANAL WINCHESTER (pt.)
THURSTON
VIOLET
WALNUT
BALTIMORE
LITHOPOLIS
CARROLL
PLEAS-ANTVILLE
RICHLAND
BLOOM
GREENFIELD
WEST RUSHVILLE
PLEAS-ANT
RUSHVILLE
AMANDA
HOCKING
LANCASTER°
FAIRFIELD
BERNE
BREMEN
RUSH CREEK
AMANDA
SUGAR GROVE
STOUTS-VILLE
MADISON
CLEARCREEK

0 2 4 6 8 10 Kilometers
0 2 4 6 8 10 Miles

N

Hidden Stories About Ohio Pioneers, Early Settlers and Their Nineteenth-Century Descendants

Peter Macklin (1794-1878), pioneer, Fairfield County, Ohio

CORNSILK
PRESS

Cornsilk Press®
Fair Oaks, California

Published by Cornsilk Press
www.cornsilkpress.com

Printed in the United States of America

First Edition: September 2022

10 9 8 7 6 5 4 3 2 1

ISBN 978-1-7364525-3-0

Library of Congress Catalog Number 2022912850

Cover and book design by Andrew Benzie
Author photo by David Navarro

PREFACE

Stories about Ohio pioneers, early settlers and their nineteenth-century descendants, stories previously hidden in family archives and public records, come to life in this collection. The narratives spotlight family strife, canal building and tragedy, opposition to a courtship, a county poorhouse, prized meerschaum pipes, a run-away child, a woman's escape from her abusive family, and the evolution of a village hotel and country schoolhouse.

The fifteen stories in this book are about my nineteenth-century ancestors who lived in central Ohio. Some of these stories kept me awake at night. Some made me smile. Others made me wish I could transport in time to talk with the principal characters.

Born in 1894 and a descendant of Ohio pioneers, my maternal grandmother Ethel Schenck Johnson just barely meets the nineteenth-century criterion. However, her story about attending a one-room rural schoolhouse and commuting by horse to the village high school just begged to be included this volume.

I know that Grandma attended a one-room school in Liberty Township, Fairfield County, Ohio because she told me so. When I was a teenager, I conducted a formal interview of Grandma. Already interested in American history and cultural anthropology, I was aware that family stories, including my family's stories, should be collected and preserved.

Grandma looked back more than half a century to describe her grade school's pot-bellied stove, students' double desks and her teachers, Mr. Sireno West and Miss Pinea Schwartz. She described her schoolgirl self (wearing a pinafore and high-top laced shoes, hair arranged in a single braid falling down her back). She recalled that she and her brother walked from their farm to their school or, in inclement weather, were transported in a horse-drawn wagon or bobsled.

I am fortunate that both my grandmother and my mother were letter writers and recordkeepers and that they were interested in family history. Their collections of assorted written materials and photographs comprise the private archives accessed for the stories in this book.

I also researched public sources (U.S. Census records, vintage maps and books, modern works about Ohio history, and genealogical databases) for information about nineteenth-century Ohio in general and my roots in particular.

I hope that you will have emotional responses to the tales in this book and that you enjoy reading each and every of them.

Sandra S. Navarro

1. STORYTELLING AND RECORDKEEPING

This book presents what I know about my mother's family's nineteenth-century history. It is based on artifacts from the past, combined with information and historical analyses from the present. You might think of this book as a collage of family stories, or perhaps a family's time capsule, which has been enhanced by current understanding of nineteenth-century Ohio.

In addition to telling stories specific to my ancestors, this book tells what life was generally like in Ohio during the 1800s. You don't have to be a relative of mine to enjoy, appreciate and learn from these absorbing stories.

The content of this book is based on what was saved as oral history (through storytelling and interviews) and what was saved as written material. The written material that has come to me from my grandmother and my mother includes letters, deeds, contracts, receipts, photographs, paper dolls, recipes, annotated almanacs, diaries, family Bibles inscribed with genealogical information, financial accounts, greeting cards, postcards, funeral cards, graduation announcements, miscellaneous household lists, articles clipped from newspapers, and notes from interviews of relatives. The paper doll on the cover of this book belonged to my grandmother. Yes, my grandmother and my mother were great savers.

The piles and boxes and drawers of memorabilia collected through the generations also include vintage cookbooks and popular fiction and nonfiction of decades past.

My maternal grandfather added to the stacks. He saved letters, military service documents and tax booklets. He wrote, then saved, articles for his village newspaper. The articles reflect his remembrances of the village as it was during his childhood and youth. A photography enthusiast, he added to the visual record of his time.

Not all the artifacts saved by my mother's family were made of paper. In addition to written items, my relatives saved objects previously used in daily life. My grandparents held on to hand-me-downs, keepsakes and ephemera from generations prior to them. Perhaps these items were cherished because they were associated with a beloved relative (meerschaum pipe, wedding ring, mourning paraphernalia). Perhaps the artifacts were saved for future use (lanterns, cooking equipment, articles of clothing), or were souvenirs of memorable occasions (photographs, travel logs, graduation announcements).

Postcard of High Street, Basil (now annexed to Baltimore), Ohio, about 1910.

I have employed my training as a cultural anthropologist and archaeologist to write several books about my maternal relatives from this assortment of items. *Ethel's Archives: A Family History from Baltimore, Ohio* focuses on my grandparents and their children. *Diary of 90-Year-Old A.E. Schenck: Pioneer Descendant in the Village of Baltimore, Ohio, 1952-1953* relates the activities, in his own words, of my great-grandfather's last year of life. My mother's records of her genealogical research anchor my book, *Chickering Read's Grave and Other Tales from 400 Years of an*

American Family. I wrote a children's book, *Visiting Great-Grandpa Read's Victorian House*, based on my memories of my grandparents' (indeed my great-grandparents') house. Written from a child's perspective, the book is about artifacts from past generations.

For this book on Ohio pioneers, early settlers and descendants, I have looked into public records for information about my relatives and the time in which they lived. As a modern anthropologist and historian, I have consulted online resources such as Ancestry.com (which provides U.S. Census data, marriage records and death records), Find a Grave (cemetery records), and Google Maps. I have researched information posted online by historical and genealogical organizations. I have looked online at out-of-print books, old newspapers and vintage maps.

These modern sources of information about the past have enhanced what my family members saved as oral tradition and tangible archival material. Interestingly, sometimes details of stories embedded in family tradition are not corroborated by these newer, outside sources.

My mother and grandmother would have been thrilled by today's methods of fact finding and fact checking. Grandma relied on the stories which came to her from her relatives, her friends and from her own direct experiences. Upon occasion, she looked in phone books when traveling in order to identify individuals with family surnames. She then visited them!

Some of Grandma's relatives were avid genealogists in the 1930s, 1940s and 1950s when information was gleaned from courthouses and other government institutions. Grandma, too, wrote government agencies (such as the Veterans Record Section, General Service Administration, Archives and Record Services, in Washington, D.C.) to obtain records.

My mother was part of this era of family history research, and while she did not travel extensively to courthouses and other record repositories, she did write to many such institutions in her search for information about her ancestors.

No matter how it is gathered, information about the past is needed when telling stories about people of the past. The preserved information influences how we understand life as it was. Not everything about everybody has been preserved or can be reconstructed. Stories are biased in this way. We may know a lot about some people, not much about others, and what we think we know may not be accurate.

Just a note here about limitations of historic records. Consider old letters. Just because somebody wrote something in a letter does not make it true or unbiased. Letters may contain misunderstandings, incomplete information, and out-and-out lies. Maybe the writer has not included parts of a story because she wants to protect her image from judgement or to protect the character of another person. Perhaps the writer does not wish to have certain information released to a correspondent or to that correspondent's social circle.

Handwritten letters can be hard to read and understand. I am thinking of the letters written in the 1890s by my great-grandmother's sister, Alice Rauch Rogers. (See Chapter 7.) I had difficulty reading Alice's handwriting, but that was not my only stumbling block. Alice wrote in pencil, and the pencil writing smeared. She used idioms and subject matter that I am not familiar with. She used words which are now archaic. As I read Great-great-aunt Alice's letters, I was often puzzled by her spelling. Her grammar and punctuation occasionally confused me. I envisioned projecting her letters on the wall in front of a group of experts for the purpose of collaborative decoding.

Just a note here about photographs. I would like to have photos of my Ohio pioneer ancestors, but I do not. Nobody does. Photography was not invented in time to catch their images. There were no photos before the 1840s and not many until decades later.

The next chapter will introduce central Ohio's Fairfield County, Liberty Township, and the Villages of Basil and Baltimore. The terms "pioneer" and "early settler" with respect to these places will be discussed.

2. PIONEERS AND EARLY SETTLERS
IN FAIRFIELD COUNTY, OHIO

T he stories in this book take place in central Ohio, specifically in Fairfield County. Neighboring counties today are Licking, Perry, Hocking, Pickaway, and Franklin Counties. The county seat of Fairfield County is Lancaster.

Fairfield County was formed in 1800.

The population of Fairfield County in 1810 was 11,361, and in 1910 it was 39,201. Not much population growth in one hundred years as you can see. During the nineteenth century (and as a matter of fact, well into the twentieth century), Fairfield County was predominantly rural. Most of its people were farmers.

Fairfield County covers an area of 509 square miles.

I like to think of the population of Fairfield County in terms of the experience of my relatives and myself. For my great-great-great-grandmother Leah Tomlinson Wisley (who was married in Fairfield County in 1806), the 1820 population of Fairfield County was 16,633. For her daughter Naomi Wisley Rauch, my great-great-grandmother, the population of Fairfield County in 1850 was 30,264. For my great-grandmother Ida Rauch Schenck, the population of Fairfield County in 1870 was 31,138. For my grandmother Ethel Schenck Johnson, the population of Fairfield County in 1910 was 39,201. For my mother (Patricia Johnson Schultz), the county's population in 1930 was 44,010, and for me, the population in 1950 was 52,130. There was a population jump in 1960, also during my childhood, to 63,912.

It is a good guess that most of us live in metropolitan areas, or counties, with populations much larger than that of Fairfield County, Ohio at any time during the nineteenth century. This might even be true for the five largest Ohio cities in the year 1900: Cleveland, 381,768; Cincinnati, 325,902; Toledo, 131,822, and Columbus, 125,560. Of these cities, Columbus is the closest to Fairfield County.

I remember the special treat of driving to Columbus during my childhood visits to Baltimore. The car trip was about 30 miles one-way. My cousin and I sat in the backseat of my grandparents' sedan. In the 1950s, there were no seatbelts, so during the long drive, we children popped up and down in play, looking through the car's rear window.

Our destination was Lazarus's Department Store where my grandmother got her hair cut in the store's beauty shop, and we children got ice cream in the store's restaurant.

Columbus had been The Destination of my mother's generation, too. In fact, Columbus was the big city that attracted Baltimore's residents during the late nineteenth century and forward in time. Letters document that Great-great-aunt Alice visited Columbus now and then in the 1890s. Her occasional trips were memorable adventures as time away from the endless drudgery of farm life in Liberty Township. My grandmother left the family's farm in Liberty Township to attend business college in Columbus in 1913. In the 1920s, her sister attended Ohio State University, also located in Columbus. Family letters document my grandfather's excursions to Columbus during the 1920s to arrange for cars to be delivered to his Ford automobile dealership in Baltimore. While trips to Columbus were fewer during the Great Depression and the years during the Second World War, my mother and her siblings also experienced Columbus as a commercial, educational and entertainment center.

Columbus's history in a nutshell follows.

Central Ohio was populated by Mingo, Shawnee, Wyandot, and Delaware people in the mid-seventeenth century. From

1663 to 1763, central Ohio was part of New France. The Treaty of Paris (1763) passed the territory to the British Empire. A Mingo village at the confluence of the Scioto and Olentangy rivers (future site of Columbus) was destroyed by Colonial militiamen in 1774. After the Revolutionary War (1775 to 1783), the area was designated as the Virginia Military District. The District attracted settlers from the East Coast. Conflict arose between these settlers and the resident Native Americans. The Battle of Fallen Timbers lead to the Treaty of Greenville in 1795. More East Coast settlers moved into the area. In 1797, an Anglo-American settlement ("Franklinton") was founded on the Scioto and Olentangy rivers. In 1801, the United States Congress set aside The Refugee Tract in the general region of future Columbus for the settlement of British Canadians who had sided with Americans during the Revolution.

The paragraph above glosses over the complex social, international, economic, and military histories of central Ohio in general and Columbus in particular. The key point is that after the American Revolution, central Ohio experienced settlement by former East Coast colonists. The settlement door opened wider after 1800. Ohio became a state in 1803.

Baltimore, Ohio, 1978 (photograph by Sandra S. Navarro).

Recordkeeping came with the presence of government. For Fairfield County, governmental recordkeeping began as follows: court cases (1800), marriages (1803), land transactions (1803), probate records (1803), census (1820), births (1867), and deaths (1867).

For this book, key locations are the Ohio villages' of Basil and Baltimore.

Basil was annexed to Baltimore on January 1, 1946. During the nineteenth century, the villages were separate and distinct. The centers of the "twin towns" were about a mile apart. Baltimore/Basil is located approximately 22 miles southeast of Columbus "as the crow flies" and approximately 30 miles by road.

Basil was named by its pioneer Swiss founders in the early 1800s after Basel, Switzerland. The village of Basil was dedicated in 1825. The village of New Market "next door" was founded by pioneer Virginians who, in the naming it in 1825, recalled their home of New Market, Virginia. In 1833, New Market became incorporated as "Baltimore."

These villages in the Pawpaw Creek Valley were along the surveyed route of the Ohio and Erie Canal. This 310-mile waterway had a significant impact on transportation and commerce for the region and state. The groundbreaking ceremony of the canal took place in 1825 at Licking Summit near Newark, Ohio about 24 miles from Baltimore, Ohio. By 1831, eight locks (each 90' by 15') had been built in the Baltimore-Basil area.

Keep in mind that the populations of the twin villages of Basil and Baltimore, Ohio were small. The population of Baltimore, Ohio in 1810 was 140. The population was 298 in 1820, and in 1830, it was 500. Looking ahead to the first decade of the twentieth century, the population of the village of Baltimore (in 1910) was 551. That of the village of Basil was 501.

In 1950, the population of the new combination of the "twin towns" was 1,843. I was a visitor to my grandparents' home in

the 1950s. My cousin and I walked to the post office to pick up the family's mail (no residential mail delivery then). Townspeople on Main Street asked me, "Are you Patty's little girl?" They knew full well that I was.

I was very surprised to be recognized. Was I a celebrity? Was my mother a celebrity? In truth, in the 1950s, many of the families of the area had hundred-year (and more) histories there. I was not a celebrity, but I was known. My identity and social connection were known. Imagine the impact this had on a five-year-old. Not only do I remember the situation of repeatedly being recognized, but I have also carried the sense of belonging to Baltimore and Basil throughout my life.

Many of the stories in this book take place in Liberty Township, Fairfield County, Ohio.

Townships are divisions of a county. Townships have some corporate powers and are found in twenty states within the United States. Ohio townships are associated with land grants and were created by the Congressional Acts which allocated sections of land for farms, schools and religious institutions. Surveyed townships were 36 square miles in size (six miles by six miles). Townships were divided into 36 numbered sections (one mile by one mile, or 640 acres in size). Beginning in 1804, Ohio townships had elected officials: three trustees, one clerk, two overseers of poor residents, highway supervisors, justices of the peace, and constables.

A business directory of Liberty Township was published in 1875 (L.H. Events and Co., *Atlas of Fairfield County*). Individuals paid a fee for their name, section number of land ownership, date settled, "nativity," post office address where mail was delivered and picked up (for instance, Basil), and business.

I have studied the list of approximately 110 names. The earliest settlement date listed is 1805, for Martin Alt. (My great-great-aunt was Ella Johnson Alt.) Six individuals on the list indicated that they settled in Liberty Township from 1805 to 1810. One of these is Peter Macklin, from Pennsylvania. Peter Macklin was my great-great-great-grandfather.

Alice Johnson Bruce, Fairfield County, Ohio, 1978
(photograph by Sandra S. Navarro).

My grandparents were undoubtedly familiar with all the names listed in the directory. They would have known the families and their stories. The directory lists many, many names that are familiar to me. I can identify J.J. Hansberger (1852, Baltimore, dealer in general merchandise); his sister was my great-grandmother Sarah Alice Hansberger Johnson. I recognize the surnames Bright, Finkbone, Fenstermaker, Geesy, Goss, Hensel, Kumler, Leonard, Langle, Norris (a family name), Roshon, Roly, Schaffner, Sager (a family name), Sutphen (a family name), and Wagner.

I know these names through having visited the village of Baltimore as a child, reading family letters during my childhood, and reading archived family letters later in life.

Not on the list from the 1875 directory are my Rauch and Schenck ancestors. I know they lived in Liberty Township. They apparently were not approached to be included in the directory, or they chose not to pay the fee. I am thankful that many of the township's people paid the fee.

A map of Liberty Township, Basil and Baltimore, Ohio was produced in 1866. Liberty Township is identified as Township 16, Range 19. Sections are delineated, and landowners (male heads of households) are identified. Many of the names in the 1875 business directory are apparent: Macklin, Sager, Bright, and the rest. I am pleased to see Rauch.

My grandfather saved a booklet, *Tax Valuation of Real Estate in Liberty Township, Fairfield County, Ohio*, dated 1910. I find Rauch relatives (my great-great-grandmother's siblings and spouses) living on section 32. There are Schenck relatives (my great-great-grandparents) living on section 15 and my great-grandparents living on section 33. In a companion publication from 1914, *List of Changes in the Assessment of Real Estate and Improvements, Mineral and Mineral Rights in Fairfield County, Liberty Township*, I spot my great-great-grandmother Sarah Macklin, and my great-great-aunt Effie Schenck Gundy, and my great-grandfather James R. Johnson.

They had roots, those relatives, that tightly secured them to Fairfield County, Liberty Township.

In summary, among the pioneers and early settlers of Fairfield County, Liberty Township, Baltimore and Basil were many of my maternal ancestors.

To clarify, these were ancestors from my mother's side of my family. My father, a child of immigrants arriving in Ohio in the early twentieth century, pointed out that his relatives waited comfortably at home in the Old Country until Ohio was up and running. Only then did they come to North America.

When I began to research Ohio's history of European settlement, I did not know or even think to distinguish between "pioneer" and "early settler." I quickly learned that among those who are passionate about the subject, there is a difference between the two terms. A pioneer has higher status in some genealogical circles than does an early settler.

According to the Fairfield County Chapter of the Ohio Genealogical Society, there are two lineage societies in the county. The Fairfield County Pioneers recognizes individuals who settled in the county prior to 1821. The Fairfield County Settlers recognizes those who settled in the county between 1821 and 1851. Members of the Fairfield County Chapter of the Ohio Genealogical Society may apply to become members of these lineage groups by submitting applications and proof of ancestry.

I am amazed at the historical and genealogical information collected, codified and preserved by the Fairfield County Chapter of the O.G.S. I am amazed at the sustained interest and enthusiasm of the members, volunteers and staff. When I say that I have conducted background research for the stories in this book, I use the term "research" in a way that would not stand muster by these passionate and dedicated individuals. My type of research is more a cruise through the historical files in order to enhance family stories.

Though I could, I am not submitting documentation for membership in the Fairfield County pioneer and early settlers lineage societies.

The log cabins of the pioneers and early settlers are long gone. While some remnants and relics of the Ohio and Erie Canal (mid-1820s to mid-1840s) still exist, today's most popular historic features in the region date from the late nineteenth century. These are covered bridges.

Fairfield County is known for having the most original covered bridges in any county in Ohio. There are now 125 historical wooden covered bridges in Ohio, and 17 of them are located in Fairfield County. One can follow the Fairfield County Covered Bridge Trail to see most of them. (Some are located on private property.) These landmarks were built in the later part of the nineteenth century.

My mother's family was fond of covered bridges. Aunt Alice Johnson Bruce commented that as a child her mother (my grandmother) and her mother's siblings played "house" and other games in and around the covered bridge which once stood near their farm on Bader Road (outside of Basil). By 1978, that covered bridge had been burned down by arsonists.

My aunt toured me to another Fairfield County covered bridge in 1978, and I took her picture posing by it. I wish I had noted the name and location of that bridge, but I did not. In comparing my photo with pictures of covered bridges currently existing in Fairfield County, I see a strong resemblance between the one in my photo to the Hizey Bridge built by J.W. Buchanan in 1891 in Pickerington, Ohio. (My relatives were linked by marriage to the Buchanans.)

The next chapter takes us to Fairfield County pioneers and will focus on Peter Macklin and his meerschaum pipes.

3. PETER MACKLIN'S MEERSCHAUM PIPES

Peter Macklin was born on February 24, 1794, in Berks County, Pennsylvania and died June 30, 1878, in Liberty Township, Fairfield County, Ohio. He is buried in the Old Basil Cemetery, Baltimore, Ohio. Peter Macklin was my great-great-great-grandfather.

I was a five-year-old exploring the parlor of my grandparents' Victorian house in Baltimore, Ohio. The family seldom used the parlor in day-to-day life. My cousin practiced her piano lessons there, but this room at the front of the house built by my great-grandfather and great-great-uncle was otherwise dark and quiet. At the time of my early childhood, the parlor primarily served as a repository for furniture and artifacts of generations past.

I liked the parlor for its seeming remoteness. Furniture there included a horsehair sofa of the Victorian era and a secretary (combination pull-down desk and glass-fronted bookshelf). The upright piano in the parlor once belonged to my great-grandmother Sarah Alice Hansberger Johnson. Photographs and paintings of ancestors hung on the walls. A framed wreath woven of human hair cut from ancestors also hung on the wall. The room held great possibilities for the curious child.

For this curious child, the two great prizes of the parlor were kept in a vase on the fireplace mantel piece. These were two long-stemmed meerschaum smoking pipes that belonged to ancestors more remote in time than my great-grandpa Alonzo E. Schenck. (A.E. Schenck was Grandma's father whom she referred to as Old Grandpa, or Grandpa Schenck, to distinguish him from my regular grandpa.)

In fact, these pipes belonged to Old Grandpa's grandfather, Peter Macklin. What was a five-year-old to do in the parlor, cut off from everyday sensibilities, but to push a chair close to the marble-fronted fireplace and retrieve the pipes from their place of protection and display? And once the pipes were in hand, what was a child to do but pretend to smoke them?

I recall the deep concern of my older cousin who knew better than I did about propriety and about my grandmother's predictable temper, should she discover my transgression.

Nearly seventy years after I deposited my DNA with his, I am in possession of Great-great-great-grandfather Peter Macklin's early nineteenth-century smoking pipes. Grandma did not find out about my mischief, and I suspect that my cousin's anxiety has long since dissipated.

A drawing of Peter Macklin exists.

I have those long-stemmed, old fashioned pipes with unadorned meerschaum bowls today. They were passed down from Great-great-great-grandpa Macklin when he died in 1878 to his daughter Sarah Macklin Schenck. The pipes were passed from Great-great-grandma Macklin when she died in 1908 to her son Alonzo Elmer Schenck. When Great-grandpa Schenk ("Old Grandpa," "Grandpa Schenck") died in 1954, the pipes came to his daughter Ethel Schenck Johnson. My grandmother died in 1968, and the pipes came to my mother, Patricia Johnson Schultz. After my mother's death in 2012, the well-travelled, two-hundred-year-old pipes came to me.

It was destined that the pipes would come to me.

Grandma told my mother that her earliest memory was of a fire that destroyed everything her family had. The fire started from a defective chimney when Grandma was just two years old (1896). She recalled that several family heirlooms survived the fire, including two meerschaum pipes that belonged to Peter Macklin, Alonzo Schenck's grandfather. Peter Macklin's gun also survived. It was passed to Alonzo's sister, Effie Schenck Gundy.

Grandpa Schenck was very fond of his grandfather's meerschaum pipes. He wrote several times in the diary which he kept at the end of his life (1952-1953) that he showed "the pipe" to his friends Charles Friedley and Mr. Roley. I am unclear about reference to the singular "the pipe," as there are two. Perhaps he carried only one to share with his friends.

Demonstrating the well-rooted nature of the community, the surnames Friedley (Friedly) and Roley appear on a document saved by Great-grandpa Schenck, that is, a list of Basil Reformed Sunday School's students and teachers in 1871.

My mother's archive of family history documents includes notes she took in 1948 during a conversation about the Macklin family. She talked with her mother and her Grandpa Schenck (whose mother was Sarah Macklin Schenck, Peter Macklin's daughter). Mom's archive also includes Grandma's handwritten notes about Peter Macklin's family and his descendants. Mom also kept notes about the Macklins as a result of her observations in Fairfield County cemeteries.

I have questions about inconsistency and incompleteness of the information in these documents, but I am not particularly troubled by the inconsistency and incompleteness. Storytelling is seldom a full and factual retelling. Even Mom's record of sleuthing in a particular cemetery cannot be assumed to be a full registration of interments there.

What is interesting is the information that the storytellers sought to preserve. Overwhelmingly, the information is about people, that is, family ties and how people fit into a three-dimensional matrix of familial relationships. Secondary themes are social description, particularly occupation (implied by land ownership) and religious affiliation (implied by church membership and burial place).

It is remarkable that Grandma knew any of this genealogical information and especially remarkable that she knew so much of it. In her 1948 conversation with my mother, Grandma relayed stories that she must have heard much earlier in her life. She was born in 1894 to the grandson of Peter Macklin. Peter Macklin died in 1878. Grandma's father (Peter Macklin's grandson, Grandpa Schenck, Old Grandpa, Alonzo E. Schenck) was only 16 years old when Peter Macklin died. I doubt that my teenager great-grandfather was the sole vessel of family history. I speculate that these stories of connection and relationship were known more widely. This accounting was essential social history of Fairfield County, Liberty Township, Basil, and possibly other neighboring locations (such as Pleasant Township).

Peter Macklin (1794-1878) (drawing from L. H. Everts, Combination Map of Fairfield County, Ohio, 1875).

The information that follows is what was recorded in these documents. I have straightened a few of the tangled threads. My additions are indicated by the use of brackets.

Peter came from Pennsylvania [Berks County] with two brothers, sisters, mother [Catherine Charlotte Miller], and father [Philip Macklin] to near (north and east of) Lancaster, Ohio [Pleasant Township, Fairfield County] about 1806 [1805] when Peter was about between 10 and 12 years old.

The children of Philip and Catherine Macklin were Peter, Betsey [Catherine? Margaret?], Sallie [Salome], Maria [Mariah], Susan [Susanna], one child deceased, Jacob, and John. Philip and Catherine Macklin were buried in Sigler, or Ziegler, Cemetery in Pleasant Township, Fairfield County.

The three Macklin brothers eventually owned about 600 acres in Pleasant Township. The Macklin brothers fell out, and Peter's two brothers bought him out.

Peter married in the east [Susanna Conklin, from Pennsylvania]. Peter had two children: Marion [Mary Ann] called Polly, and Uncle Phil [Philip].

Polly married David Harter. Polly and David Harter had two sons and a daughter. They lived at Dumontville, Ohio and ran a hotel on the toll road to Lancaster.

Peter's first wife [Susanna Conklin Macklin] died. [She died when her child Philip was six weeks old, and Philip was raised by his grandparents, Philip Macklin and Catherine Miller Macklin.] Susanna Conklin Macklin was buried in a little cemetery on Rt. 37 at Olive Church [Sigler or Ziegler cemetery, Pleasant Township, Fairfield County].

The children of Philip's (Uncle Phil's) first marriage were Polly (who married Mr. Reese), Gilia [Gela] (pretty girl who married Mr. Alt), Susie (who married Mr. Mauger), Media [Almeta] (red-headed, mean girl who married someone at Pataskala), unidentified girl who married Mr. Yeager [Yager] and went to Illinois, unidentified girl who married Mr. Sharer, Perry who married Lallie Smurr, Peter who married Miss Feeman, and an unidentified offspring who married Weasner. Philip was married a second time to Mrs. Feeman who had two children (Leanie and Willis Feeman). Philip and Mrs. Feeman had a son Charley who married a Reelhorn. Philip Macklin married a third time (unidentified woman), but they had no children.

For the record, the following paragraph from *The Biographical Record of Fairfield and Perry Counties, Ohio,* published by S.J. Clarke Publishing Company in 1902, provides the information that my grandmother could not recall.

> In 1847 Mr. Macklin was united in marriage to Miss Sarah Radabaugh and to them 13 children were born, 8 of whom still survive. Peter, a resident of Pleasant Township, Fairfield Co.; Perry who is living with his father; Arvilla, the wife of John Dreeher of Columbus; Susan, the wife of Samuel Mauger of Liberty Township; Polly, the wife of Charles Reese of Basil; Octavia, the wife of Henry Weisner of Pleasant Township; Gela, the wife of Daniel Alt of Liberty Township; Almeta, the wife of Isaac Maslin who is living in Licking Co., Ohio; Mrs. Martha Montgomery, deceased; Victorine, the wife of Henry Smoke; Selena, the wife of Lewis Sheer of Illinois; Sarah Ann, the widow of Henry Yager; and one that died in infancy...Philip Macklin married a second time, Mrs. Jane Feeman and the third time to Mrs. Susan Saliday."

In the paragraph above, I (insider by association) recognize the surnames Mauger, Weisner (Weasner), Alt, Yager, and Saliday.

It is very telling that Grandma, who had a very keen memory for ancestral connections and relatives' names, could not provide the full list of her Uncle Phil's people. This suggests that that branch of the family was not particularly important to her. It could be because Uncle Phil was brought up by his grandparents and not by his father Peter (and his father's second wife Barbara), that feelings of kinship were weak.

Grandma continued:

> Then Peter Macklin married Barbara Doomy [1828]. They moved out on Ridge Road where he had bought a lot of acreage [SE eighth (80 acres) of Section 16 in

Liberty Township]. There was a little log cabin there, and he later built onto it. This is where Earl Andreggs [meaning, the Earl Andregg family] now live. [Earl Andregg was the son of John Andregg and Samantha Macklin Andregg.]

Peter and Barbara's children were Amos, Maria [Anna Maria], Sarah, Sophie, Caroline (called Cal), Sophie [Sophia], and Selene. There was also Samantha.

Amos married Liddie Harter who taught one term of school. They had four children. Maria married Jim Buchanan, and they had five children (Peter, Cecelia, Julian, Charles, and a girl who died very young). Sarah married David Schenck, and they had nine children (Dellie who married Dan Rance, Lillie who married George Swartz, Ada who married William Hughes, Alonzo who married Ida Rauch, Willie who died in childhood, Effie who married Silas Gundy, Ernest who died in childhood, Maude who married Verle Good, and Olin who married Ettie Heimberger). Sophie married John Andregg and only lived six or seven months afterwards. Selene married Dave Weasner and had five or six children. Caroline (or Cal) married Charlie Sims. Cal and Charlie had about nine children including Leafie, Charlie, Martin, Rollo, Earnest, and Clarence. Samantha [half-sister?] married John Andregg, and they had four children (Ida who married Phalsgraf, Harl who married x, Josie who married Will Allen, and Earle who married Linnie Berry).

It appears that after the death of his first wife Sophia Macklin, John Andregg married Samantha, Sophia's half-sister.

Ethel recalled what happened to Peter Macklin's 325 acres, "125 acres to Philip as the oldest son (Polly Harter's share in money), 20 acres to Weasners (later owned by Doc White), 20 acres to Buchanans (on west of Doc White's piece), 80 acres (homeplace to John Andregg), 20 acres to Sarah, 35 acres to

Amos, 17 acres to Cal (later owned by the May family), and 8 acres to Big Ide ('Cal's girl')."

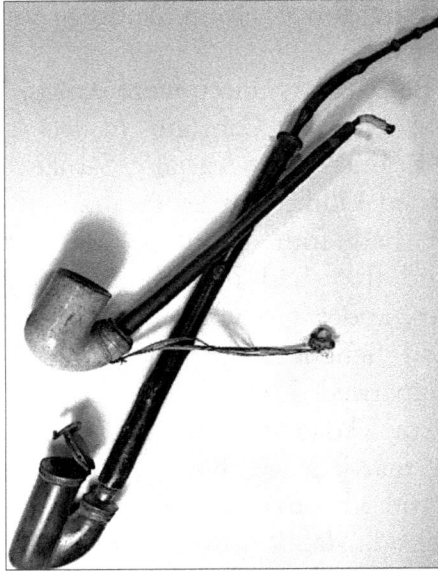

Peter Macklin's meerschaum pipes, 2022 (photograph by Sandra S. Navarro).

Grandpa Schenck was also part of that 1948 conversation with my mother and grandmother. Here's what Grandpa Schenck added to the story about his grandfather Peter Macklin, owner of the meerschaum pipes: Peter Macklin lived to be 84. He is buried at the Basil Cemetery [Old Basil Cemetery] with his second wife, Barbara. They went to the Reformed Church.

Some final notes on the Macklins concludes this chapter. It is the Macklins' back story. The Macklins were really Mechlings.

Tad Deffler's website (www.geocities.com/tdeffler/mechling) is an excellent source on the Mechling/Mechlin/Macklin family tree. There are more than 20,000 individuals listed in this tree. My grandmother would have been delighted with this database.

Theobald Dewalt Mechling, born about 1701 in Germany, died April 1765 in Bucks County, Pennsylvania and was buried near Dillingerville, Pennsylvania. The records show that he was a tanner and a farmer. He arrived in Philadelphia on September 11, 1728, on the ship "James Goodwill" from Rotterdam via England. The ship arrived in America on June 15, 1728. Theobald traveled with his brother Jacob from, probably, the Lower Palatinate or Lower Alsace area.

Philip Macklin (father of Peter Macklin) was the son of John Peter Mechling, son of Theobald Mechling. I am descended from John Peter Mechling, the second son of Theobald Dewalt Mechling. Philip Macklin changed his surname from Mechling to Macklin.

Despite all the family connections outlined in this chapter and many who are listed on the modern database, I am the one to have inherited Peter Macklin's meerschaum pipes.

4. DAVID FRANKLIN SCHENCK'S CHILDHOOD TRAUMA

David Franklin Schenck was born on December 29, 1832, in New Jersey and died on April 15, 1927, in Ohio. He is buried in Old Basil Cemetery, Baltimore, Ohio. David Franklin Schenck was my great-great-grandfather.

David Franklin Schenck was born in New Jersey on December 29, 1832, and moved to Fairfield County, Ohio as a child. On January 30, 1854, he married Sarah Ann Macklin, daughter of Peter and Barbara Doomy Macklin. From Sarah's parents, David and Sarah were deeded land in Range 19, Township 16 (Liberty Township), Section 15, of Fairfield County. Eight of David and Sarah's ten children survived into adulthood. David died on April 15, 1927, at the age of 94 years, three months and sixteen days.

The facts of David Franklin Schenck's happy marriage to a pioneer descendent, his many offspring, and his long life in Fairfield County do not reflect the suffering he experienced as a young boy.

He was uprooted from his early childhood home in New Jersey when his family moved to Ohio. His father died. His mother remarried, and the newly constituted family moved from David's Ohio home to Indiana. His mother died. His stepfather remarried. David was mistreated by his stepparents. He ran away from Indiana, back 163 miles to Fairfield County, Ohio.

I don't know David's age when he ran away from Indiana. I speculate his age to be about 11 (assuming he ran away in 1843). The family story describes David as a boy when he made his way back to Fairfield County. The year of David's mother's death is unknown, but Grandpa Schenck said his grandmother died at a young age.

David Franklin Schenck (1832-1927).

My grandmother tucked into her desk drawer handwritten notes about her grandfather David Franklin Schenck. The sketchy notes record the following.

David Franklin Schenck's father, William Schenck, was a shipbuilder. His sister Kitty was a milliner and had a large millinery store in New Brunswick, New Jersey.

William Schenck married Sarah Demut [Demuth, DeMuth] Sutphen. Sarah's brothers were Richard and James Sutphen. William Schenck and the Sutphens came from Somerset County, New Jersey. William Schenck and Sarah Sutphen Schenck had two children: Sarah Elizabeth (Libby) and David Franklin Schenck.

William and Sarah Sutphen Schenck traveled to Ohio in a covered wagon with their two children. [Probably Sarah's two brothers Richard and James were already in Fairfield County.] Sarah was a good horsewoman. They lived at Emma Griley's site. [The Griley House is the Baltimore Community Museum in Baltimore, Ohio.] William Schenck died. Sarah married a second husband. Sarah went west to Indiana, near Fort Wayne [Decatur] where she died.

My mother's notes report the story, as follows:

Sarah DeMuth Sutphen Schenck was Grandpa Schenck's grandmother, wife of William Schenck, mother of David F. Schenck. She is buried near Ft. Wayne, Indiana in a cemetery near the depot. When her husband, William Schenck, died, she married again. Was his name Cheney? They had 100 acres of farmland near Decatur in her name. David Franklin, her son, went out there to live as a child, but when his mother died, he was mistreated by his stepfather (who had married again), and he ran off and came back to Basil. Later he returned to try to claim his mother's land but failed. He took Grandpa Schenck along with him on one trip. Mother said Grandpa Schenck used to speak of "Uncle Dick Sutphen," possibly the R.D. Sutphen mentioned on Premium List of fair winners of 1851.

Grandma's brother and sister accompanied their father Alonzo Schenck to Indiana in April 1918. They wrote in a letter to Grandma (dated April 2, 1918) that they were going to Decatur, Indiana to visit "dad's grandmother's grave." Decatur is about 20 miles from Ft. Wayne. My mother's notes Sarah Sutphen Schenck was buried near Ft. Wayne.

Mom searched the Fairfield County marriage records, 1803 through 1865, and found some Sutphens. They are: 1833,

Richard Sutphen and Sarah Perele; 1834, James Sutphen and Sarah Williams.

My grandmother's and mother's notes are all that remain of the story of William Schenck and Sarah DeMuth Stuphen Schenck Cheney. Clarifying information from modern databases eludes me.

David Franklin Schenck returned to the place of his childhood (Basil, Ohio) where he had relatives (Uncle Dick Stuphen).

U.S. Census records from 1860 forward state that David Franklin Schenck was living in Liberty Township until his death in 1927. His wife Sarah Macklin Schenck died in 1908. In 1920, he lived with his son Olin and Olin's wife Etta. (The modern database says that David Franklin Schenck lived on Ridge Road, Liberty Township, Fairfield County, Ohio with son Alan, but the son was Grandpa Schenck's brother James Olin, always called Olin.)

My aunt Alice Johnson Bruce wrote in a letter (dated December 1978): "David Franklin Schenck died at age 94 after an accident on his farm. He was senile and sawed off a limb of an apple tree while sitting on it, breaking his hip, from which he never recovered. But he was hardy. He used to hike into town to buy supplies twice per week, two miles each way and an extra mile over to see Granddaughter Ethel and her family. Mother always made homemade biscuits for 'old Grandpa' every Saturday morning, knowing he would be at our house for noon lunch!"

From his obituary saved by his descendants, I learn that David Franklin Schenck was a member of Trinity Reformed Church, Basil, Ohio. "Although he was unable to hear a word of singing or of the sermon, yet his place was in the Lord's House on the Lord's Day, and he thus set before his children and those who shall follow him a noble example. It is possible to sit quietly in the Church and receive a blessing."

David Franklin Schenck (1832-1927).

A brief announcement in the local newspaper at the time of his death said that David Franklin Schenck was believed to be the oldest man in Fairfield County.

He would not have had that distinction had he not run away, travelling 163 miles from his abusive stepparents in Decatur, Indiana to his Uncle Dick Sutphen in Fairfield County, Ohio.

5. RAUCH FAMILY'S PERPETUAL NAMESAKE

Philip Rauch was born on December 9, 1784, in Berkshire County, Pennsylvania and died on March 19, 1841. He is buried in the Bright Cemetery, Fairfield County, Ohio. Philip Rauch was my great-great-great-grandfather.

The perpetual namesake of the pioneer Rauch family is Rauch Road. What follows is the story of Philip Rauch, my great-great-great-grandfather. (The family pronounced their surname "Rau," the final "ch" being silent.)

Rauch Road is located in Liberty Township, Fairfield County, Ohio. Rauch Road Northwest (written NW) is near Bader Road NW and Basil Western Road NW and Leonard Road NW. Landmarks in the area are the John Bright Bridge (a covered bridge over Fetters Run in Lancaster, Ohio), Baltimore Campground (an historical site), Old Basil Cemetery, Mount Carmel Cemetery, the villages of Carroll and Dumontville, and the waterways of Poplar Creek and Pawpaw Creek.

My Rauch ancestors had connections to the Bader family, the Leonard family and the Bright family. A Schenck relative ran the hotel on the toll road in Dumontville, and my Schenck grandparents lived in Carroll at one time. The creeks noted above fed the Ohio and Erie canal which my ancestor Schuyler Van Ransler Johnson helped build in Baltimore, Ohio in the early 1830s. Many of my ancestors are buried in the Old Basil Cemetery, including some Rauch ancestors.

Philip Rauch was born in Berkshire County, Pennsylvania in late 1785. He came to Ohio with his father George Rauch (a Revolutionary War veteran) and his mother Mary Rauch in 1806 or 1807. Philip was 21 years old and was Philip and Mary's youngest son. The family lived in vicinity of Lancaster for a few months, but they soon resettled in Liberty Township.

George and his wife Mary Rauch transferred their interest in their Liberty Township farm (located in Section 28) to Philip in 1814. Philip married Susannah Alspaugh in 1818, and the couple had eleven children. The farm passed to Philip's fourth child, John (my great-great-grandfather). John married Naomi Wisley. The couple had ten children. My great-grandmother Ida Rauch Schenck was their nineth child. She grew up on the ancestral farm.

Country road in Liberty Township, Ohio, early 1950s (photo by Harry R. Johnson).

By the way, Susannah Alpaugh's family was in Fairfield County, Ohio in 1808. Another pioneer lineage.

Philip Rauch was a soldier in the War of 1812.

My grandmother knew that her great-grandfather Philip Rauch was a veteran of the War of 1812.

In 1951, Grandma wrote a letter of inquiry to the Chief of Veterans Record Section, General Service Administration, Archives and Record Services, Washington, D.C., seeking information on Philip's service and pension records.

The Chief of the Veteran's Records Section, Arthur H. Leavitt, replied on March 9, 1951. His letter is reproduced here:

This is in reply to your request of January 22, 1951. Among the bounty-land records in the National Archives is a file cited as above (BL wt. 87 123-160-55).

Parents: Not mentioned.

Birth: December 9, 1784, place not shown.

Family: The veteran married Susanna (also shown as Susanah and Susannah) Alspaugh or Alspauch on October 8, 1818, in Fairfield County, Ohio. Susanah was born on January 25, 1799. The veteran and his wife had the following children: George, born on August 10, 1819; Elizabeth, born on February 15, 1821; Sarah, born on August 27, 1823; John, born on March 10, 1825; Andrew, born on May 25, 1827; Delila (also known as Delia, Delilah), born on September 8, 1829; David, born on December 21, 1831; Jacob, born on February 26, 1835; Philip, Jr., born on June 21, 1837; and Mariann (also known as Mary Ann) and Emanuel, twins, born on July 26, 1841. The last four mentioned children, referred to as the minor children of the veteran, were living in 1858. Jacob, son of the veteran, was living in Fairfield County in 1858. It is stated in a family record that George Rauch died on October 22, 1820, relationship to the veteran not stated. No further discernible family data are given.

Residence: Fairfield County, Ohio, during service. It was also stated that the veteran lived there at the time of his marriage and was still residing there at the time of his death.

Death: The veteran died on March 19, 1841, in Fairfield County. Susannah Rauch, widow of the veteran, died on January 30, 1847, in Fairfield County.

Service: When application for bounty land was made on behalf of the minor heirs of Philip Rauch, it was stated that the veteran served from about September or October 1, 1813, until about February, March or May 1, 1814, as Private with the Ohio Militia under Captain Joseph W. Ross and Colonel John Delong. It was likewise stated that the veteran was discharged at Fort Shelby in Detroit.

Bounty Land: Warrant No. 87,123 for 160 acres of bounty land was issued under the Act of March 3, 1855, to Jacob Rauch, Philip (Junior) Rauch, Emanuel Rauch and Mary Ann Rauch, minor children of Philip Rauch, on account of the service of the veteran in the War of 1812.

I have deciphered the complicated puzzle of Rauch family in my book, *Chickering Read's Grave and Other Tales From 400 Years of an American Family*. Here is a sample paragraph:

The correspondence helps to clarify questions about Rauch family members. Susanna's first and maiden names have varying spelling in the records. National Archives record says that Emanuel (Emmanuel), the twin brother of Mollie, was alive in 1858. (He would have been about seventeen years old.) "Mollie," Emmanuel's twin, was Mariann or Mary Ann (or Mary A. in her obituary). Susanna outlived her husband Philip by about six years. Deliah (Delia, Delila, Delilah) was not the oldest Rauch daughter. (It was Elizabeth.) After her mother's death in 1847, Deliah likely did not care for the older offspring (George, age 28; Elizabeth, age 26; Sarah, age 24; John, age 22; Andrew, age 20). Possibly she cared for David, age 16; Jacob, age 12; Philip, Jr., age 10; and Emanuel, age 6. (Mollie, or Mary Ann, was said to live with John.)

Without notes such as these, I am lost. Deliah, Mollie and John appear in this book in Chapter 7.

By the way, Sarah Rauch (third child of Philip and Susannah Alspaugh Rauch) married Peter Bright. Philip Rauch and Susannah Alspaugh Rauch are buried in the Bright Cemetery.

In Fairfield County, many roads and landmarks carry names of pioneers and early settlers. Although early nineteenth-century family ties may be forgotten today, Rauch Road still winds through the fields of Liberty Township.

6. IDA RAUCH SCHENCK'S FAMILY STRIFE

Ida Rauch Schenck (Mary Ida Rauch Schenck) was born on September 30, 1864, in Liberty Township, Fairfield County, Ohio and died on May 9, 1939. She is buried in Old Basil Cemetery, Baltimore, Ohio. Ida Rauch Schenck was my great-grandmother.

On February 8, 1899, Charley Rauch wrote a letter to his older sister Ida, "Well, Sister, sad but true, Mother is dead, ten 'til two, and the funeral is Saturday at ten, Mt. Carmel. This is all. Rev. D. will preach if we can get him. Good bye, Chas. Rauch."

"Mother is dead." Naomi Wisley Rauch was dead.

With this message, the painful relationship between Great-grandma Ida and her parents might have ended, but the ache of Rauch family strife continued throughout Ida's life.

Ida Rauch Schenck passed away in 1939 at the age of 75. My mother's 1948 field notes on her Rauch ancestors contain information from an interview with Grandma, daughter of Ida Rauch Schenck. My grandmother told my mother that many of Ida's siblings were "mostly no account," except for Perry. Ida's emotion was carried forward three generations to me.

Looking back, the men of my Rauch lineage in Fairfield County, Ohio are: (1) John Rauch (Ida's father, prosperous farmer and civic leader) who was the son of (2) Philip Rauch (Ida's grandfather, War of 1812 soldier, Ohio pioneer) who was the son of (3) George Rauch Ida's great-grandfather, Revolutionary War soldier, Ohio pioneer).

Ida had deep roots in Liberty Township. Her great-grandfather George Rauch owned land in Section 28 which he passed to his heirs. Ida's father John Rauch owned the Section

28 farm and acquired additional land in Section 29. By 1870, he held 350 acres.

The Rauch farm located in Section 28 was about three and a half miles from what was then the village of Basil, now the western part of Baltimore, Ohio. The Rauch property was located south of the intersection of Bader Road NW and Leonard Road NW. Section 29 is to the west of Section 28 and bisected by Havensport Road NW. Poplar Creek runs through Section 29.

Ida was born in 1864. In 1870, Ida's father (township treasurer and township trustee) built what was described as a "handsome family residence." As a six-year-old child, Ida would have known that her family had lived at this location for sixty years. When her mother died, Ida would have known that her family had lived at this location for more than ninety years.

I am able to trace conflict in Rauch family letters. On October 21, 1891, Ida's older sister Alice wrote to her future brother-on-law Alonzo (Lon, Lonnie) Schenck, "It just plucks the heart out of me, the way my people act, but what can I do but let them run their race. I can't see sometimes how Ida can endure it much longer." She continues, "I glory in your bravery."

Great-grandpa Alonzo Schenck and Ida Rauch were married in March 1892. I believe that Ida's parents objected to their courtship.

On November 20, 1891 (during her visit to her Aunt Deliah Parmalee in St. Louis), Alice wrote again to Lon: "It does one good to hear you don't give an inch for the people down there. Just stand up for your rights. They have tried to run over you long enough, and by what I understand, they haven't got very far yet. I often think of my little brother and sister. Last night I was thinking about the past and about the pebbles coming up at the window."

Pebbles thrown by Lon to attract his sweetheart Ida's attention.

Alice's letters document the declining health of her father John, beginning in August 1894. Relatives, neighbors and friends came to pay their respects, to assist with John and to aid in the functioning of the household and farm. Alice wrote, "More people here in the last two weeks than in the past five years."

John Rauch lingered in extremely poor health for seven months.

On April 6, 1895, Ida's brother Charley wrote, "Dear Sister Ida, Pa is worse and not expected to live very long. Will send for the rest of the children. There was nothing said about sending for you, but I am going to see Mother about it. See what she has to say. I am going to Carroll to telephone for Alice."

Ida Rauch Schenck (1864-1939).

By this time, Alice was married and living with in Columbus, Ohio with her new husband, George Rogers.

Charley added as a later postscript to the letter, "Mother said you didn't belong to the family."

On April 10, 1895, George Rogers wrote to Lon and Ida, "I don't know if you know about Ida's father's death. They sent for Alice last Saturday. He died Monday. His funeral was today. I lived in hopes there would be a change on behalf of you folks, but it seems there was no change."

Soon after George Rogers' letter, Alice wrote Ida, "They haven't mentioned your name to me since I've been home and don't think they intend to send for you, not even any word. This I consider a scandalous disgrace."

Ida saved a newspaper clipping, "Will of John Rauch" (not dated, no source indicated):

> The will of the venerable John Rauch, late of Liberty township, was admitted to probate last Thursday at 10 o'clock.
>
> He gives to his wife, Naomi Rauch, in lieu of her dower, the farm on which they now reside, in Liberty township, containing about 250 acres, during her natural life. He also gives to his wife, absolutely, certain personal property, which is specifically enumerated.
>
> He authorizes his executors to sell the remainder of his real estate in Liberty township, being about 70 acres in section No. 29 and about 20 acres in section No. 28, at private sale, for not less than $50 per acre. He provides, however, that if they are unable to sell said real estate at such price, they shall sell the same at public sale in separate tracts to be sold in either case within two years. He provides, with any other moneys arising from other sources, after the payment of all debts and the legacy of $260, as follows:
>
> To Louisa Rutherford, his daughter, one-seventh; to his son, Andrew Rauch, one-seventh, less the amount of a certain note, with interest, he holds against said son; to his daughter-in-law, Minerva Rauch, wife of his son Jeremiah Rauch, one-seventh, less the amount of a certain note held against him; to his daughter, Alice M.

Rauch, one-seventh; to his daughter, Ida Schenck, one-seventh.

To his son Oliver P. Rauch, one-seventh, and to his son, Charles Rauch, one-seventh. After the death of his said wife he authorizes his executors to sell the lands devised to her, at public sale in two tracts, the half section line dividing the same. The proceeds to be equally divided among his seven children as above stipulated with all other funds arising in said estate.

Jeremiah Rauch and Charles Rauch are named as executors without bond under the will. The will is dated January 13, 1894. E.F. Holland and Cora A. Holland are the attesting witnesses.

Letters testamentary were issued to the executors, who estimated the personal property to be work about $1,500 and the real estate about $17,500. Total estimated value of the estate, $19,000.

Here are the players:

> Naomi Wisley Rauch (John's wife)
> Louisa Rauch, born in 1851
> (married to Adam Rutherford)
> Andrew Rauch, born in 1853
> (married to Matilda Boyles)
> Jeremiah Rauch, born in 1856
> (married to Minerva Looker)
> Oliver Perry Rauch, born in 1857
> (married to Minnie Bader)
> Alice Rauch, born in 1862
> (married to George Rogers after John's death)
> Ida Rauch, born in 1864
> (married to Alonzo E. Schenck)
> Charles Rauch, born in 1868
> (never married)

Ida also saved a "testified copy of will" (or certified copy) dated April 18, 1895. The will itself is dated January 13, 1894.

John left Naomi personal property: "Three horses, two cows, one buggy, one set of buggy harnesses, one double set of work harnesses, one iron plow, one corn plow, one copper kettle, two iron kettles, one 2-horse wagon, one grind stone, two hundred bushels of corn, sufficient hay to feed three horses until new hay is made, two hundred dollars in money, all the household goods, furniture and provisions contained in my dwelling house cellar and summer kitchen and all the growing wheat (if any) at the time of my death in the tract devised to her."

Gravestones of Naomi Wisley Rauch (1829-1899) and John Rauch (1825-1895), Bright Cemetery, Baltimore, Ohio.

John gave to his son Oliver Perry Rauch the sum of $260.

The will differs from the newspaper account in saying that there are 79 acres in Section 29 to sell (rather than 70).

The payment of debts referred to in the newspaper clipping refers to funeral expenses and administrative costs. His son Andrew owed him $75.00 and $137 (since March 11, 1880), plus six percent interest. Minerva (wife of Jeremiah) owed John $393 (since January 1, 1892), plus six percent interest. Note that John's wife Naomi inherited use of the land only; after her death, the land was to be sold at public sale, then one seventh given to each son and daughter (with Andrew and Minerva still paying their debts to John's estate).

It is interesting that John left inheritance to his daughter-in-law Minerva, rather than his son Jeremiah. Jeremiah is named as one of the executors, as is son Charles. Charles was willed his one seventh part.

Why would John designate Jeremiah an executor, given the large amount of money owed by Jeremiah to John?

A letter in my family archive summarizes the situation of John's estate. Ida's sister-in-law (Perry's wife, Minnie Bader Rauch) wrote to Ida and Ida's husband Alonzo from Marion, Ohio on February 10, 1898. Note that this letter is dated four years after John Rauch's death and that Naomi Rauch was still living.

> Sister Ida and Lon and Babies, Perry said I should write you a few lines this morning for him. He was too tired last night to write, in reference to this way things are going in home, in the settling up of the estate. He never can get any satisfaction out of them fellows Jerry and Charles. We never know anything, only what we got around about way. Never will tell us anything. Never even told us that the farm was sold. We got it in newspaper. Allie wrote to us several weeks ago in reference to them and wondered if you four heirs couldn't make the fellows give bond, meaning you, Rutherfords, Allie, and Perry making the 4 heirs. So Perry wrote a nice letter to Jerry and asked him what they had done and what they was doing and what they

were going to do. He said Jerry, I would like to know once what you and Charles are doing and have a satisfaction once. And he wrote Perry the most meanest and awful letter you ever read. We sent it to Allie and let her read it. She was surprised to read such a letter. He just give it to Perry and Rutherford. Perry has taken it in hands now and he says he is going to find out what they have been doing. And he don't intend to ask J.M. or Charles anymore about it. He wrote to the Probate Judge and to the Sheriff for information (at Lancaster). I copied the letters he wrote and sent them to Allie and told her to send them to you and Lon. Suppose you have received them by this time. We have an answer from the Sheriff. Perry said I should copy it and send it to you folks. I sent a copy to Allie yesterday. But we haven't heard from the Judge yet. Perry said if he did not get an answer soon, he was going to write to Sq. Holland of Basil and have him look the matter up for him and see what is wrong.

Now Ida and Lon, if you get to see Adam Rutherfords you tell them all about what Perry is doing and post them as we haven't wrote to them yet. It makes us so much writing. You post them. Tell them Perry wants them to stay with him and if you can make them fellows give bond or step down and out and let someone else take their place, that can give satisfaction. You heirs had better get things out of their hands now if you can. Then let them go on if they don't get to give it to you this time, they will make it up the last pull. But you see the money from farm is in the Sheriff's hands and now we feel so much easy than if it was in their hands. I suppose the Sheriff has put the money in bank. Now you know if that bank should happen to fail, you heirs would all lose your money, every cent of it unless you would be able to prove that the Sheriff knew when he deposited that the bank was not safe. Then you could make the Sheriff and his bondsman stand good for it. Perry thinks it will be alright though. But of course, you never can tell nowadays as there is so many banks closing. Enclosed here you will find a copy of the Sheriff's letter.

Here is what Sheriff J.W. Steward (Lancaster, Ohio) wrote to Perry on February 4, 1898:

Dear Sir, In reply to yours of recent date, will say the 79 62/100 tract sold to Jacob Reaf for $34.00 per acre amounting to $2,707.08. The twenty acres tract sold to Samuel L. Bader for $30.00 per acre amounting to $600. Total amount of $3,307.08. Amount of cash received on day of sale $1.100.36. Court cost $81.80. Taxes $66.60. Attorney's fees $119.23 deducted from first payment leaving a net balance of cash in my hands of $846.23. There has not been any distribution yet. Cannot tell you why. You understand the deferred payments will be in one and two years. Each payment $1102.86 which will be increased by the interest at 6%. This is all the information I can give you at present as I know nothing about the heirs' share. I presume that Atty. J.M. Wright will make the distribution soon. Hoping this will be satisfactory. Will close. Yours truly,

The sale of the land was at a price far less than the price stipulated in John's will.

Naomi died four years after John's death.

Ida's brother Charles wrote to Ida on February 15, 1899, a week after's his mother's death:

Well, Sister, this morning I thought would write you and give you the news. Well, I got your letter this morning and I thought I would write right away. They divided the bedding and the dishes among all of us, and the pictures and her clothes was divided among you girls.

Now I would like to know what I am to do with your things. So I will take care of them till I see you or hear from you. The rest of them leave their kit packed and ready to go. Alla is going home tomorrow, and Perry is going too I guess so they are all gone but me. Well, I tell you I am pretty well fixed. I got the dog and the dog house left. They couldn't divide him for he wouldn't come. Well, when there is a will there is a way. I am going to close for this time. Will tell you the rest when I see you. You will have to excuse this working paper. This was all I had."

Ida saved two cardboard-backed portrait photos (studio-produced "cabinet cards") of her older sister Alice (known as Allie and Alla) and two of her younger brother Charles (known as Charley and Roxy). In 1918 when she and Lon took a cross-country road trip in their new Hudson Super Six, they visited Ida's older brother Perry and his wife Minnie at their home in Palacios, Texas.

There is no evidence of Ida's reconciliation with her brother Jerry or documentation of her association with her sister Louisa or brother Andrew.

I know that my grandmother knew Jerry's children because in September 1951 she wrote to my mother concerning a genealogical question: "I could also contact my dear (?) cousin Florence Rauch Kindler, Jerry's eldest daughter. I might have bumped into her last Saturday if I had accepted the invitation I received to attend the meeting of the Bright Cemetery Association, but I went to Columbus instead."

Ethel's cousin Florence was about three years older than Ethel. The same letter revealed that Grandma knew where her Uncle Charley lived but that she had little contact with him.

Thus Ida's family strife continued.

7. ALICE RAUCH ROGERS' BURDENS AND DESPAIR

Alice Rauch Rogers was born on August 18, 1862, in Liberty Township, Fairfield County, Ohio and died June 15, 1926. She is buried at Wesley Chapel Cemetery, Hilliard, Franklin County, Ohio. Alice Rauch Rogers was my great-great-aunt (my great-grandmother Ida Rauch Schenck's) older sister.

Alice Rauch was two years older than her sister Ida. Alice was six years older than her brother Charley (known affectionately as Roxy). These three were the youngest of the ten children born to John Rauch and Naomi Wisley Rauch.

Alice Rauch Rogers (1862-1926).

Alice and Ida corresponded with each other beginning in October 1891 when 29-year-old Alice went to visit Aunt Delia Rauch Parmalee in St. Louis, Missouri and Aunt Mollie Rauch Morgan in Bluffton, Indiana. This lengthy trip was so significant that Ida noted Alice's homecoming in her 1892 almanac, "Alice came home from St. Louis, 10 of February." (The almanac is an advertiser for J.A. Kumler's pharmacy in Baltimore, Ohio, "Drugs, Medicines, Chemicals, Fine Toilet Soaps, Brushes, Combs, Etc., Fancy Articles, Perfumery in Great Variety, Physicians' Prescriptions Carefully Dispensed, Fine Cigars and Tobacco.")

While Alice's letters are hard to read because of her handwriting, spelling, use of archaic words, and her choice of a pencil as a writing instrument, it is clear that Alice's visits to her relatives in Missouri and Indiana were made in desperation. Alice was away from her home for four months for a greatly needed rest from the burdens and tedium of farm life. She also sought escape from stress imposed on her by her parents and brother Jerry.

When Alice left on her trip, Ida still lived with their parents. Shortly after Alice's return, Ida left the Rauch farm when she married Alonzo Schenck. Did Ida seek escape too?

Excerpts from Alice's letters to Ida and Alonzo follow.

Alice Rauch (from St. Louis, Missouri) to Ida Rauch, October 11, 1891:

> I am getting over the idea of trying to do everything to save a cent. Life is too short. There is good wages for girls who sew. Here they pay $12 per month for help [housework]. Going to get fancy work to do and going to Exposition. No scolding here.

Alice Rauch (from St. Louis, Missouri) to Alonzo Schenck, October 21, 1891:

SANDRA S. NAVARRO 49

It just plucks the heart out of one, the way my people act. But what can I do but let them run their race. I can't see sometimes how Ida can endure it much longer. I glory in your bravery. I can never go home and stay unless things change. How is Brother George Rogers?

This is Alice's first mention of George Rogers, a friend of Lon's. In 1891, George was a married man.

Alice Rauch (St. Louis, Missouri) to Ida Rauch, November 21, 1891:

Got your money order. Got a letter from Ida and Stella [nieces] telling about Perry [Alice and Ida's brother]. Why under the sun don't they get a girl [this is a reference to a paid helper] till I come home? Has the doctor been to see Mother? I was not surprised to hear of Papa's sickness. I never had better health. Sometimes I feel I had ought to be at Home, then again, I think I can't sacrifice all my pleasure for them when I don't feel that I am appreciated. Parmalees want me to learn dressmaking. They want me to get into something.

Alice Rauch (from St. Louis, Missouri) to Alonzo Schenck, November 20, 1891:

It does one good to hear you don't give an inch for the people down there. Just stand up for your rights. They have tried to run over you long enough and by what I understand, they haven't got very far yet. I often think of my little brother and sister. Last night was thinking about the past and about the pebbles coming up at the window.

Alice Rauch (from St. Louis, Missouri) to Alonzo Schenck, December 29, 1891:

Talks about gifts: a beautiful jewelry box and two kerchiefs. And all I could eat of everything that was to be had in the city Christmas Eve. Made candy and cracked nuts. Went to a play, dancing party, church, spiritualist lecture. (It was the most laughable thing). Going to visit Aunt Mollie.

Alice Rauch (from St. Louis, Missouri) to Alonzo Schenck, January 6, 1892:

Obliged to you for the money. Our friendship is growing stronger every day and when you and Ida gets settled and they don't treat me any better than they have, I will come and make my home with you and Ida. I surely can earn my board and clothes. They are just begging me to stay here and says if they don't do better by you when you go home, just come back. Will come home and help sister get out. I think the sooner you and Ida get out, the better.

The January 6, 1892 letter suggests that Alonzo may have lived on the Rauch farm.

Alice Rauch (from St. Louis, Missouri) to Alonzo Schenck, no date:

Guess I will have to come home and help. Don't think I will stay. They will have to be better to me than ever before. Ida told me all your plans. Aunty will send something nice for the marriage.

Alice Rauch (from Bluffton, Indiana) to Ida Rauch, February 4, 1892:

This has been the happiest time in all my life. I expect to look back over the past four months in years to come with much pleasure. This is the hardest task for me to leave this city. Big-hearted people.

Alice Rauch (from Bluffton, Indiana) to Ida Rauch, February 5, 1892:

She [Mollie Rauch Morgan] is a lively auntie. Minnie and her husband are just splendid. Home next week. Roxy at the station.

These letters were sent to Basil, Ohio. This puzzled me at first. Ida lived with her parents on the farm in Liberty Township. I thought Alonzo (Lon) lived with his parents in Liberty Township. (In fact, there are clues that Alonzo lived on the Rauch farm.) In 1891 and 1892, letters were mailed to the post office where individuals then picked up their mail. "Rural Free Delivery" was not part of the Post Office Department's services until 1902.

Postcard of Market Street, looking west, Basil (now annexed to Baltimore), about 1910.

I was also initially confused that Alice was writing to Lon rather than to solely to Ida. I suspect that Alice was writing to Lon in order that her letters not be read in by others in the

Rauch household. Alice left her homeplace to escape turmoil. Her aunts knew this. Aunt Delia Rauch Parmalee not only entertained her niece, but she sought to help her identify a means to establish a home and means of support away from John and Naomi Rauch. The letters record Alice's skill in sewing, and Alice seriously considered whether or not she can support herself as a seamstress.

At the end of her four months of respite, however, Alice returned to Liberty Township. Roxy picked her up at the Basil train station. I picture her in the wagon with him, happy to see her younger brother but apprehensive about going back to the Rauch family farm.

Homecoming was not the end of Alice's dissatisfaction and unhappiness. Ida married Lon in early March 1892. Without Ida's help, Alice faced more work on the Rauch farm. She had experienced city life and the kindness of her aunts and their families. More letters from Alice to Ida written in 1894 confirm this.

Alice Rauch (from Rauch farm) to Ida Rauch Schenck (Marcy, Ohio), February 18, 1894:

> I have a 2-week wash and want to make a kettle of soap. Had ague back. Went to bed with the headache. Mother had the sick headache.
>
> How is the baby? Have you named her yet? I wish I was close enough that I could run in every day to see you. Don't expect to set down until the roads get good in the spring. I don't expect to get away very much until I go for good which may be at no far distant day. I have already gave them the benefits of the best part of my life.

Alice Rauch (from Rauch farm) to Ida Rauch Schenck (Marcy, Ohio), February 28, 1894:

> Baked bread this forenoon. We have got our feather bed renovated. We have all the ticks to sew up. We got

18 yards new ticking. Made pillows. I don't want another job of that soon. I have 5 new calico dresses. I made one for Mam. Took in quarterly meeting. Old Den Langel is to be buried tomorrow. People with mumps. Have you found a name for the baby yet?

Alice Rauch (from Rauch farm) to Ida Rauch Schenck (Marcy, Ohio), March 18, 1894:

> I must go and milk cows. Had a fresh cow while I was in Columbus. Am raising the calf. It's raining. Can't wash, so will make Mother another new calico dress.
>
> [Alice wants to see Ida but has to wait until the spring work is done.] I will have to do everything myself. They won't hire anyone unless I pay them. I said I would see them across the sea before I would do that. I told them just what I would do and what I would not do.
>
> When is our friend George Rogers coming down to visit your baby? I will be lucky enough to happen there about the same time.

Alice mentions George Rogers, "our friend," now a widower.

Alice's letters say that she met George Rogers at a camp meeting, a popular type of Protestant outdoor gathering in the nineteenth century. The Lancaster camp meeting began in 1872, originally in Logan, Ohio, then in Carroll, Ohio for several years. The Lancaster camp meeting relocated to its current site in Lancaster, Ohio in 1878. It is referred to as The Lancaster Camp Ground. In 1892, the Chautauqua Movement added to the institution's Christian foundation. Celebrities such as William Jennings Bryan and President William McKinley spoke to assemblies of thousands there.

Alice Rauch (from Rauch farm) to Ida Rauch Schenck (Marcy, Ohio), April 1, 1894:

To Baltimore and Basil yesterday, to get dress. Ripped up old back silk dolman and will have a cape made. Ida Rutherford [niece of Alice and Ida, the daughter of their older sister Louisa] is coming to stay a few weeks. Will finish a quilt this week. In box are tomatoes, peppers, strawberries. Have 30 chickens and nine dozen eggs last week. Five pounds of butter. Had a steer to sell for $25. Will shove the money down my pant leg for future use.

Alice worked hard on the farm, and part of her labor was directed toward providing for her future. She raised a steer, sold it and kept the earnings "for future use." Alice, 32 years old, had not accepted a future for herself as a permanent worker on her parents' farm.

Alice Rauch (from Rauch farm) to Ida Rauch Schenck (Marcy, Ohio), May 31, 1894:

Sent Baby a pair of shoes and hood. Went to Bethel quarterly meeting Sunday. Going to Basil. I am so missing a house of my own. Remaking a dress.

Alice Rauch (from Rauch farm) to Ida Rauch Schenck (Marcy, Ohio), June 19, 1894:

Jim C. was drowned last eve in Walnut Creek near Cap Brandt's. It seems to be a shock in the neighborhood and surely a warning to all. The day nor the hour, no one knoweth how soon they will be called. So I think it best to be prepared. Life is short at best. It seems I've hardly begun to live.

Alice Rauch (from Rauch farm) to Ida Schenck (Marcy, Ohio), June 26, 1894:

Got a washing machine and ordered an ironing board. The washing I have to do, I need a machine. Set out celery. Chickens and eggs, plums, grapes, apples. Can't come [to visit Ida] before camp meeting.

I have seen a drawing of a Wayne combination rocker motion washing machine, patented in 1883. It is a wooden box on four legs which was filled with water and agitated by hand. In 1894, Mildred Lord was granted a patent for a washing machine that was a tub on legs which was agitated by a crank. This was an improvement over the tub and wash board. While Alice bought an ironing board, she still had lots of work to do with a flat iron which weighed five pounds and was heated on the wood-burning stove.

Alice Rauch (from Rauch farm) to Ida Rauch Schenck (Marcy, Ohio), July 17, 1894:

Regarding George Rogers, I have been studying the subject for several months. He isn't the prettiest man I ever saw, but pretty is as pretty does. I haven't seen him since at camp [camp meeting] about four years or more.

In August 1894, John Rauch became quite sick. Alice's work and anxiety increased with all the visitors and helpers who came to the Rauch farm.

Alice Rauch (from Rauch farm) to Ida Rauch Schenck (Marcy, Ohio), September 7, 1894:

Thrashers came yesterday, 22 for dinner and 23 for supper. Aunt Mollie here. Pap is no better. The end will soon come. I have been tied down so long, I almost feel like I am in jail. Give my best to friend George Rogers.

Alice Rauch (from Rauch farm) to Ida Rauch Schenck (Marcy, Ohio), September 25, 1894:

Mother will stay up with him tonight. He is getting some better. Dr. Brown thinks he can patch him up to last a while. He is getting childish. [Aunt Mollie is visiting and invited Alice to stay with her in Indiana, mentioning that Alice would get $1 daily pay for "serving."] I have so many advisors, I hardly know which to listen to. I have met so many traitors in my short lifetime that I feel like almost living a secluded life. I trust no one.

Maybe I expect too much. Give my regards to friend George, trusting we will remain friends.

Alice Rauch (from Rauch farm) to Ida Rauch Schenck (Marcy, Ohio), October 1, 1894:

[Alice wants to hire a "girl," meaning someone to help her with the household and garden.] I am not going to be tied down and work day and night just to save a few cents for somebody else. Pap can't walk now nor do one thing.

Alice Rauch (from Rauch farm) to Ida Rauch Schenck (Marcy, Ohio), October 21, 1894:

He is no better and never will be. He said today he had made up his mind; he would have to go the trip before long. Went to the fair [Fairfield County Fair]. I was somewhat disappointed not seeing friend George R. at the fair as built high hopes on having a talk with him. You can tell him I would like very much to see him. He can come here, but I have so little time to entertain. Lots of company. Am husking corn.

Alice Rauch (from Rauch farm) to Ida Rauch Schenck (Marcy, Ohio), October 30, 1894:

I would rather live in a log cabin. I want a peaceable and quiet home of my own.

Alice Rauch (from Rauch farm) to Ida Rauch Schenck (Marcy, Ohio), November 11, 1894:

I had a nice letter from our friend GLR. He has lots of confidence in Charley and Jerry. (Stayed with them.) [This is a reference to Alice and Ida's brothers who are named executors for their father's estate.] He seems to feel very sorry that our meeting was so short, and he requests that we meet again soon. How old is he, do you know? Dad is getting very light. People are staying nights with him.

Alice Rauch (from Rauch farm) to Ida Rauch Schenck (Marcy, Ohio), December 7, 1894:

Hardly know what to do regarding George Rogers.

Alice went to see George Rogers in Columbus where he had a store ("Rogers and Reed, Dealers in Fresh and Salt Meats, Vegetables, Flour and Feed; Corner of Harrison and Fourth Avenues, Columbus, Ohio"). George was previously married to Laura B. Dildine. They were married in 1883. Laura died in 1893 at age 32, leaving behind a son (Cecil) and a daughter (Lucile).

Alice wrote Ida that she liked George's house. She confirmed that George had two children living at home. Alice asked Ida for advice on what to do.

Alice Rauch (from Rauch farm) to Ida Rauch Schenck (Marcy, Ohio), January 20, 1895:

Waiting to hear what you had to say in regard to me leaving the hills. I see nothing in staying here any longer. Dirty drudgery. I don't think they will give me very much after all my work and long stay with them. George Rogers is a little undersized and not the prettiest man in the world.

Alice Rauch (from Rauch farm) to Ida Rauch Schenck (Marcy, Ohio), February 10, 1895:

> I had a letter from George Rogers saying that he and Roxy had quite a racket but was coming down. I am anxious to get off the hill.

Alice Rauch (from Rauch farm) to Ida Rauch Schenck (Marcy, Ohio), March 8, 1895:

> Butchered 5 hogs. Pap is no better.

Alice Rauch married George Rogers in mid-March 1895. John Rauch died in April 1895.

Alice Rauch Rogers (Marble Cliff, Ohio) to Ida Rauch Schenck (Marcy, Ohio), July 5, 1896:

> As happy as a woodpecker on a sweet cherry tree. Pleasant 4th of July. George, Lucile and I and Charley and Jennie and Sama Reed all went out to Minerva Park.

George and Alice had a farm in addition to their store. The Rogers grew wheat and hay on their farm. Alice writes about milking ten cows with George and Cecil and about the plentiful gooseberries, raspberries, apples, pickles, and eggs. Camp meetings continue to be an important part of their lives.

"As happy as a woodpecker on a sweet cherry tree," Alice found the peaceable, quiet home of her wishes.

8. CHARLEY RAUCH'S MYSTERIOUS LIFE

C harles "Charley" Rauch was born on August 11, 1868, in Liberty Township, Fairfield County, Ohio and died on June 25, 1953, in Fairfield County, Ohio. Charley Rauch was my great-grandmother's (Ida Rauch Schenck's) younger brother.

My grandmother's letter to my mother (September 21, 1951) says, "I have a notion to go down to County Infirmary and see Uncle Chas. Rauch someday. So far as I know, he is still living. And he might be able to give me some dope on family connections." (Both my grandmother and mother were conducting genealogical research at that time.)

Charles Rauch (1865-1953).

I do not know if Grandma acted on her intentions to "go down to County Infirmary and see Uncle Chas. Rauch someday." I suspect not as there is no record of such a visit in Mom's collection of Grandma's letters from 1951 and 1952. By late June 1953, Grandma would have missed her opportunity to get "some dope on family connections."

Alonzo Schenck's diary entry for June 26, 1953, says, "Charlie Rauch passed away today and in paper." My great-grandfather knew Charley as his wife Ida's younger brother. Charley had been a welcome visitor to the Schenck household.

Charley's obituary in the *Lancaster Eagle Gazette* (June 26, 1953) reads, "Charles Rauch, 89, for eleven and one-half years a resident of Fairfield County Home, there died Thursday, 6:30 p.m. A former resident of Havensport community, Mr. Rauch's only survivors are nieces and nephews. Services will be held Monday 2 p.m. in the James H. Sheridan Sons funeral home, with Rev. Anthony Ruble of Good Shepard Chapel officiating, Havensport. Friends may call at the funeral home after today."

Charles Rauch is listed on the 1870 U.S. Census record as a one-year-old living with his parents John and Naomi in Liberty Township, Fairfield County, Ohio. The other children in the household are Louisa (age 18), Andrew (age 17), Jeremiah (age 14), Oliver P. (age 12), Alice (age 7), and Mary (later known as Ida, age 5). All the children except for Louise and Charles attended school.

Charles was known as Charley and Roxy.

In the 1880 U.S. Census, Louisa had married and moved away from the farm, leaving Andrew (age 27), Jerry (age 24), Perry (age 22), Alice (age 17), Ida (age 15), and Charles (age 11).

In the 1900 U.S. Census, thirty-year-old Charles is listed as living with his brother Jerry and sister-in-law Minerva. Jerry and Minerva had two children (eleven-year-old Bryon and nine-year-old Florence). They lived in Basil (Liberty Township, with a Basil address), Fairfield County, Ohio. Charley's occupation is recorded as "farmer."

Charles Rauch (1865-1953).

According to the 1910 U.S. Census, Charley Rauch (now 42) lived with Jerry and Minnie still, in Liberty Township. Bryon is not listed, but Florence is listed (now nineteen). Jerry and Minnie have a second daughter, Esther (age seven).

My mother's genealogical field notes record three Rauch graves in the Bright Cemetery, Fairfield County: Bryon A. Rauch (son, born 1888, died 1908), Minerva Rauch (mother, born 1860, died 1919), and Jerry Rauch (father, born 1856, died 1930).

I do not know what happened to Charley during the dozen years after the death of his brother Jerry in 1930 and when Charley moved to the Fairfield County Home in 1941 or 1942. He was described in the newspaper obituary as an unmarried resident of Havensport community during those years.

The *Lancaster Eagle Gazette* obituary tells us that Charley lived to be 89, that he lived at the Fairfield County Home (previously known as Fairfield County Infirmary) for eleven and a half years. Charley would have been 78 when he moved to the Infirmary.

The main structure of the Fairfield County Infirmary opened in 1828. The Infirmary underwent remodeling and expansion during the 160 years that it was a county institution. (The Fairfield County Infirmary closed in 1985.) Outbuildings were added to the property, and adjacent farmland was purchased to provide food for the residents. In 1917, natural gas lines were installed for heating and lighting. In 1926, water pipes were added, replacing reliance on a natural spring and groundwater.

The main infirmary building was used as a hospital and as a "poorhouse." There were public charges, paying patients, patients with mental illness, homeless patients, and elderly residents.

Alice Rauch Rogers wrote to her sister Ida Schenck on August 9, 1896: "Was Rox and Allie down to [barn] raising? Did he say when he was coming up? This is his birthday. It don't seem hardly possible that he is 28 years old today. I remember as well as it was but yesterday when he was born."

Attaining the age of 89 in 1953, Roxy outlived both Alice (who died in 1926) and Ida (who died in 1939).

9. OLIVER SHEPARD READ'S GENERAL STORES

Oliver Shepard Read was born on May 21, 1804, in Attleboro, Massachusetts and died on March 15, 1882, in Franklin County, Ohio. He is buried in Green Lawn Cemetery, Columbus, Franklin County, Ohio. He was my great-great-great-uncle.

My mother's Great-aunt Mattie Johnson (Martha Broyles Johnson) wrote to Mom on March 30, 1950:

> Dear Pat, this is the first spare time I've had since receiving your welcome letter, to write and tell you how much I appreciate the information you gave me of the Read family. I'm quite sure they first settled in Baltimore [Ohio] for Grandpa [John Shepard Johnson] said his Grandfather Read [Oliver Read, Jr.] helped make the brick to build Baltimore's first hotel which was the old brick building which stood between Humler's drug store and Kauffman's house. It is now torn down. Henry and I owned it at one time, and Harold was born there.
>
> Uncle Shepard Read owned and operated a store on the corner where Osborn's store was. That was back more than a hundred years ago when Baltimore depended on the canal for shipping grain and other commodities.
>
> I think when Shepard Read [Oliver Shepard Read] left Baltimore, he first went to Reynoldsburg, and it was during that time his father Oliver Read went to Blacklick.

My Great-great-aunt Mattie is recounting the development of Baltimore, Ohio in the 1830s and 1840s, "back more than a hundred years ago when Baltimore depended on the canal for shipping grain and other commodities." The Ohio and Erie Canal was built adjacent to Baltimore in the 1830s.

The 1830 U.S. Census records Oliver S. Reed [Read] living in Walnut, Fairfield County, Ohio. Ohio marriage records say that Oliver Shepard Read married Mahala Warner on March 1, 1837.

Oliver Shepard Read was an early merchant in Baltimore, Ohio. Aunt Mattie's letter tells us that Oliver Shepard Read was known as "Shepard Read." I suspect that this was so because there were so many Olivers among the Reads that to clarify who was who, he was known by his middle name. Back home, that is, back home several generations in Connecticut, that strategy wouldn't have helped as many carried the name Shepard as either first or last name.

Postcard of Main Street, Baltimore, Ohio, about 1910.

I care very much about the Olivers, Shepards and Reads because of one particular person: Chickering Read Read.

Chickering had a double last name. Chickering was born on August 5, 1778, in Wrentham, Massachusetts. Chickering and Oliver Read, Jr. were married in Wrentham, Massachusetts on March 26, 1801. (Oliver Read, Jr. was born on March 4, 1773, in Pomfret, Connecticut.)

Their first child, Nancy Read, was born on December 30, 1801, at Wrentham, Massachusetts. Their second child, Oliver Shepard Read, was born in Attleborough (Attleboro), Massachusetts on May 21, 1804. Their third child, George Albert Read, was born in Cumberland Hill, Rhode Island on August 4, 1808. Their fourth child, Caroline Chickering Read, was born in 1810, possibly in Cumberland Hill, and died in 1811. Their fifth and last child, Mary Eliza Read, was born on August 21, 1815, in Walpole, Massachusetts.

During or after 1815, the family moved from Massachusetts. A comment in my mother's notes say they moved from Wrentham to Baltimore, Maryland and from there to Baltimore, Ohio. A distant cousin, William Hannum, believed that they moved to Columbus, Ohio in 1815.

Chickering Read was the mother of Nancy Read Johnson who was the mother of John Shepard Johnson who was the father of James Read Johnson who was the father of Harry Raymond Johnson. Harry was my grandfather.

Chickering Read was a real relative. She was family. As a seven-year-old, I practiced saying her relationship to me. She was my great-great-great-great-grandmother.

The story of Chickering and Oliver Read has fascinated me from the time I was a little child at the knees of my genealogy-loving mother and grandmother. The intriguing question to them and so to me was: where was Chickering Read's grave? We actually took excursions to cemeteries to look for Chickering Read's grave.

Aunt Mattie thought Chickering Read must have been buried in Blacklick, Ohio. Blacklick is a small unincorporated community in southern Jefferson Township, Franklin County, in the Columbus metropolitan area.

Modern databases have solved the mystery. The grave of Chickering Read Read is located in Walnut Hill Cemetery, Columbus, Franklin County, Ohio. She died at the age of 44 on October 13, 1822.

Grandma and Mom focused on Chickering's husband Oliver Read because he was the son of one of our Revolutionary War ancestors, also named Oliver Read. Oliver Read, Sr. served in the Woodstock Company in the Lexington Alarm, in April 1775. He enlisted on March 10, 1775, as a private and later served as a sergeant in the company commanded by Capt. Stephen Brown of Woodstock, 4th Regiment, Connecticut. He was "omitted from the rolls" in November 1778 when he was supposed dead.

Son Oliver Read, Jr. was born in 1773 before Oliver Read's enlistment. He did not know his father who was "omitted from the rolls." (There is more to the story which can be read in full in my book, *Chickering Read's Grave and Other Tales From 400 Years of an American Family.*)

At the age of seven, I was not only interested in the whereabouts of my great-great-great-great-grandmother's grave, I was interested in her migration story. She moved from Massachusetts to Ohio with my great-great-great-great-grandfather and their four children. I had made several moves by that time in my life, so we shared something in common.

While the Read emigration story focuses on Franklin County, Ohio, I was focused on Fairfield County, Ohio. That was the ancestral home in my mind, and, indeed, Chickering Read's son Oliver Shepard Read lived in Baltimore and had a store there.

Oliver S. Read is mentioned in C.M.L. Wiseman's *Pioneer Period and Pioneer People of Fairfield County, Ohio*, published in 1909, as follows: "Joseph H. Ijams established a general store in Baltimore, Ohio, about 1838, in which Oliver S. Reed [Read] was a partner and who had previously been in the employ as a clerk with Michael Ruffner first and William Wing afterward and who died in the city of Columbus several years since."

This is the store that Aunt Mattie mentioned in her 1950 letter, "Uncle Shepard Read owned and operated a store on the corner where Osborn's store was."

The 1850 U.S. Census record from Baltimore, Fairfield County, Ohio states that Oliver Shepard Read, age 46, was married to Mahala. Living with them was his father, Oliver Read (husband of Chickering).

The Reynoldsburg-Truro Historical Society's website informs readers that Reynoldsburg was named for James C. Reynolds, a settler there about 1831. He opened a general store that supplied provisions to the builders of the Cumberland Road (the National Road, U.S. Route 40). James C. Reynolds is said to have been the first merchant in the area. He died in 1854.

It is possible that Uncle Shepard Read, a merchant, understood the commercial possibilities of Reynoldsburg. At the same time, he understood the commercial decline of Basil and Baltimore as shipping began to move away from canal transportation to railroads. His parents had emigrated from Connecticut to Franklin County, Ohio in 1815, said our distant cousin William Hannum. At any rate, Shepard, Mahala and Oliver Read moved to Franklin County between 1855 and 1860.

The distance between Baltimore and Reynoldsburg is 18 miles.

The 1860 U.S. Census records Oliver Shepard Read (identified as a retired merchant) and Mahala Read in Reynoldsburg, Franklin County, Ohio. Oliver Read, Shepard's 86-year-old father, lived in the household.

The 1880 U.S. Census records Oliver Shepard Read (identified as a publisher) and Mahala living in Columbus, Franklin County, Ohio.

Oliver Shepard Read and Mahala Warner Read had eleven children, seven of them born in Baltimore, Ohio and four born in Reynoldsburg, Ohio. My great-great-aunt Mattie knew Rosa Alice Read, Uncle Shepard's daughter, who was born on February 17, 1858, in Reynoldsburg. Rosa was a generation older than my grandfather (Harry R. Johnson), her distant cousin. They shared ancestors (Oliver and Chickering Read) but did not share a sense of close kinship.

To my great-grandfather James Read Johnson, Oliver Shepard Read was "Uncle Shepard." I am certain (for reasons given in the next chapter) that James Read Johnson thought very highly of his great-uncle.

10. SCHUYLER VAN RANSLER JOHNSON'S CANAL
BUILDING AND TRAGEDY

Schuyler Van Ransler Johnson was born on April 4, 1803, in Dutchess County, New York and died on October 15, 1841, in Logansport, Cass County, Indiana. He is buried in Ninth Street Cemetery, Logansport. He was my great-great-great-grandfather.

Schuyler Van Ransler Johnson was the first of my Johnson relatives to live in Baltimore, Ohio. He migrated to Ohio from Dutchess County, New York. He married Nancy Read in Hamilton Township, Franklin County, Ohio on March 18, 1827. Schuyler was 24 years old; Nancy was 25 years old.

Nancy was introduced in Chapter 9 as the daughter of Oliver and Chickering Read. The Read family emigrated to Ohio from New England about 1815.

There has always been confusion within my mother's family as to whether or not Oliver and Chickering Read lived in Baltimore, Ohio (Fairfield County) or near Columbus, Ohio (Franklin County). The marriage between Schuyler and Nancy in Franklin County would suggest that the Reads lived in Franklin County.

We know that Chickering Read died in 1822 and was buried in Franklin County. We also know that Oliver Read lived with his son Oliver Shepard Read in Baltimore (Fairfield County) in 1850 and later with this same son in Franklin County.

It seems that everyone in the family was right about the location of the Reads' domicile, though they may have been confused about sequence and timing.

*Remains of Ohio and Erie Canal lock, near Baltimore, Ohio, 1953
(photo by Harry R. Johnson).*

Schuyler Van Ransler Johnson worked as a stone cutter (or lock cutter) on the construction of the Ohio and Erie Canal. I suspect that Schuyler had been a stone cutter in New York. The great Erie Canal in upstate New York was completed in 1825. The second-longest canal in the world (China's Grand Canal was longer), the Erie Canal connected the Great Lakes Basin to the Atlantic Ocean. When work on the Erie Canal was completed, Schuyler followed the work of stone cutting (for the canal's locks) to Ohio.

The groundbreaking ceremony of the Ohio and Erie Canal took place in 1825 at Licking Summit near Newark, Ohio (about 24 miles from Baltimore, Ohio).

Schuyler and Nancy's first child, John Shepard Johnson, was born on December 6, 1827, in Newark, Ohio.

It was no surprise that Schuyler and Nancy moved to Baltimore, Ohio from Newark. The proposed route of the Ohio and Erie Canal was surveyed in 1822. The Pawpaw Creek Valley villages of Baltimore, Ohio and Basil, Ohio were along the 310-mile surveyed route of the Ohio and Erie Canal. Again, Schuyler followed the work of stone cutting.

It is certain that Schuyler Johnson and Nancy Read Johnson lived in Baltimore, Ohio in the early 1830s. Schuyler, it is said, built a log cabin in Baltimore. I know this because my Johnson grandparents lived at the site of the log cabin on South Main Street when they married in 1916. Their house was built on the foundation of Schuyler and Nancy's cabin.

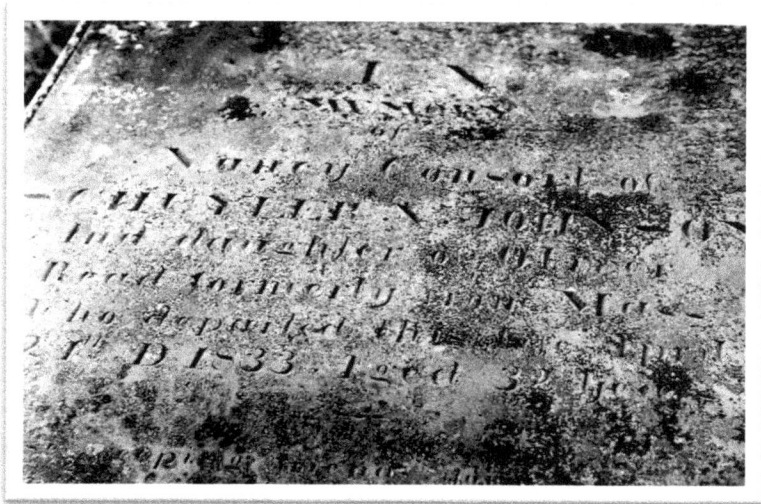

Table gravestone of Nancy Read Johnson, wife of Schuyler van Ransler Johnson, Old Basil Cemetery, Baltimore, Ohio. "In Memory of Nancy, consort of Schuyler V. Johnson and daughter of Oliver Read, formerly from Mass., who departed this day, April 24, 1833. Aged 32 years." (photograph by Vincent Schultz, 1949).

Grandma and Grandpa knew Grandpa's great-grandparents' story.

Aunt Martha "Mattie" Broyles Johnson shared this information in a letter (dated March 30, 1950) to her grandniece (my mother), "Grandpa Johnson's [John Shepard Johnson's] mother [Nancy Read Johnson] died in the house where you children were born. It was a log cabin of only two rooms. So, you see, the Johnsons have been there a long time."

Schuyler and Nancy had three children: John Shepard Johnson (born on December 6, 1827, in Newark, Licking County, Ohio), George Van Ransler Johnson (born on September 11, 1830, in Baltimore, Fairfield County, Ohio) and Nancy Chickering Johnson (born on March 23, 1833, in Baltimore, Ohio). All three children were given family names: Shepard, Van Ransler (a variation of Van Rensselaer, an historic and well-known name in New York) and Chickering.

Baby Nancy Chickering was one month old when her mother Nancy died on April 24, 1833. It is tempting to suggest that Nancy died of causes related to childbirth.

House at site of Nancy Read Johnson's log cabin, Baltimore, Ohio (photograph by Sandra S. Navarro, 1978).

My mother made observations at the Old Basil Cemetery of Nancy's tabletop tombstone on October 6, 1949. Mom transcribed the inscription in her notebook, "In Memory of

Nancy, consort of Schuyler V. Johnson and daughter of Oliver Read, formerly from Mass., who departed this day April 24, 1833. Aged 32 years." My father took at picture of this old tombstone in the fall of 1949.

Life expectancy for individuals born in the year 1850 in the United States has been calculated. White males born in 1850 could expect to live to age 38. White females born in 1850 could expect to live to age 40. In comparison, both Schuyler and Nancy were born about the year 1800. Nancy lived to age 32. Schuyler lived to age 38.

Baby Nancy Chickering died on August 9, 1833, at about 4 months old and was buried in Old Basil Cemetery. The baby died three months after the death of her mother.

My mother's great-aunt Ella Johnson Alt provided family history information in a letter (dated October 11, 1948) to Mom's father, Harry R. Johnson. Pat copied Aunt Ella's letter in a notebook. An excerpt reads, "The row of stones by the Table are some of the Reads."

By 1831, eight canal locks (each 90' by 15') had been built in the Baltimore-Basil area. By the time of Nancy's death in April 1833, Schuyler's stone cutting work might have reached a slow down or an end. Schuyler followed canal building work to Logansport, Indiana. Logansport, the county seat of Cass County, was organized in 1828. Logansport's population in 1830 was 1,262, jumping to 5,480 in 1840. It seems that others were drawn to the canal's construction and the commerce it generated during this time period.

The distance between Baltimore, Ohio and Logansport, Indiana is 240 miles.

Great-great-aunt Ella certainly knew why Schuyler moved to Logansport, Indiana: work could be obtained in the construction of the Wabash and Erie Canal. The Wabash and Erie Canal was part of a canal and river system that eventually linked the Great Lakes to the Gulf of Mexico. Construction of the canal reached Logansport, located on the Wabash River, in 1837.

My great-great-aunt Ella's letter says that Schuyler Van Ransler Johnson died in Logansport, Indiana, Cass County, October 15, 1841, and that he was buried there. An online search of Logansport cemetery records found that "S. V. Johnson" was buried in Ninth St. Cemetery. He was 38 years old when he died.

Records of Logansport's Ninth St. Cemetery also document the grave of Schuyler's second wife, "Consort Phebe Johnson, 36 yrs., 6 months, 11 days." Her date of death is not provided.

Great-great-aunt Mattie's letter to my mother (November 15, 1949) states, "Grandpa [John Shepard Johnson] said he knew he had a half-sister but never kept in touch with the family after his father's death."

Schuyler's second wife may have lived for some time after Schuyler's death. We know she had at least one child with Schuyler. She may have remarried. She may have had more children.

Mattie's letter continues, "Grandpa Johnson [John Shepard Johnson] never had any records of the Johnson family that I know of, and I've never located his father's grave, have never been in Logansport but once, although I've inquired several times of people whom I have met from there if they ever saw a table tombstone in any of the old cemeteries; one person thought he had seen such a stone but was not sure."

"Grandpa Johnson" referred to by Mattie was John Shepard Johnson, the first of Schuyler and Nancy's children. He carried the name of his Shepard ancestors, Revolutionary War "patriots" in Connecticut. John Shepard Johnson was my grandfather's grandfather. My grandfather Harry R. Johnson knew his grandfather John Shepard Johnson, and there are photos of John Shepard Johnson in the Johnson photograph collection.

By now, readers must be wondering happened to the two children of Schuyler van Ransler Johnson and Nancy Read Johnson when Schuyler, a widower, moved 240 miles from

Baltimore, Ohio to Logansport, Indiana, to follow his trade of stone cutting.

This very question kept me awake many nights, 190 years after the fact. I will address it in Chapter 11.

11. JOHN SHEPARD JOHNSON'S ABANDONMENT STORY

John Shepard Johnson was born on December 6, 1827, in Newark, Licking County, Ohio and died on July 29, 1915. He is buried in Old Basil Cemetery, Baltimore, Ohio. John Shepard Johnson was my great-great-grandfather.

John Shepard Johnson is reachable to me. I can envision his relationship to me. He was my grandfather's grandfather, a connection which is far easier to imagine and say than counting out the "greats." I know what he looked like in his senior years as there are photographs of him in the Johnson photo archive.

I also know that he had grey eyes, dark hair, a dark complexion and was five feet six inches tall. I know this because in 1964, my grandfather, Harry R. Johnson, sent me his grandfather's volunteer enlistment paper for service during the Civil War:

I, John S. Johnson, born in Newark in the State of Ohio, aged thirty-six years and by occupation a plasterer, do hereby acknowledge to have volunteered this twelfth day of February 1864, to serve as a soldier in the Army of the United State of America, for the period of three years, unless sooner discharged by proper authority."

By the time of his enlistment, he had been married to Isabella (Bell) Norris Johnson for 14 years and had a house full of children. Knowing that he married, had a family and lived nearly eighty-eight years in his hometown created a picture of this relative far different than the tragic story of abandonment by his father.

I should have picked up the clue to the story of John Shepard Johnson's abandonment in Great-great-aunt Mattie's letter to my mother (November 15, 1949): "Grandpa [John Shepard Johnson] said he knew he had a half-sister but never kept in touch with the family after his father's death."

John Shepard Johnson did not live with his father Schuyler Van Ransler Johnson. Schuyler, the stone cutter for great canals, left John and his younger brother George in Baltimore, Ohio when he moved to Logansport, Indiana. Guessing that Schuyler left Baltimore in 1833, little John would have been about six years old. His younger brother George would have been about three. Baby Nancy Chickering was already buried in Old Basil Cemetery next to her mother's grave.

Schuyler, the potentially unemployed stone cutter, experiencing the loss of his young wife and their baby, left town and his two children for a location 240 miles away. I doubt that he ever saw his boys again. He remarried and died within the decade, in Cass County, Indiana.

When the facts meshed to become a story, I literally lost sleep over the fate of these two small boys.

Aunt Ella was John Shepard Johnson's daughter. Aunt Mattie was his daughter-in-law (wife of John's son, Henry Irvin Johnson). Neither of these aunts conveyed a sense of alarm or anguish in their letters about their father's childhood. There are only two clues.

The first clue has already been mentioned. From Aunt Mattie, we learn that although John Shepard Johnson knew about his half-sister and step mother in Logansport, Indiana, he did not keep in contact with them after his father's death. (John would have been 13 years old at the time of his father's death.)

The second clue also comes from Aunt Mattie, that John Shepard Johnson did not keep any records of his Johnson relatives.

He disassociated with Schuyler who abandoned him and his toddler brother.

John Shepard Johnson (1827-1915).

Nobody is alive to tell me for certain who took care of the boys, John and George. I believe it was their mother's brother, Oliver Shepard Read.

Oliver Shepard Read's story was told in Chapter 9. Oliver Shepard Read was the son of Oliver Read and Chickering Read. They emigrated to Ohio with their children in about 1815. Oliver Shepard Read married Mahala Warner on March 1, 1837, and their first child was born in 1838. Oliver Shepard Read is mentioned in C.M.L. Wiseman's 1909 book, *Pioneer Period and Pioneer People of Fairfield County, Ohio*, as owning a general store in Baltimore, Ohio about 1838.

Assuming Schuyler van Ransler Johnson left for Indiana in 1833, did his bachelor brother-in-law care for the two boys?

John Shepard Johnson was Oliver Shepard Read's (Uncle Shepard's) namesake. What other answer can there be?

John Shepard Johnson lived in Baltimore, Ohio for nearly nine decades. His early childhood trauma did not seem to affect his personal or community life. Harry R. Johnson (John's grandson) wrote: "My grandfather worked at various times at a [Baltimore, Ohio] warehouse at water's edge on the south side of the local canal basin, helping to load the out-bound boats with grain. I remember him saying that, on several occasions, he had seen a solid line of teams, with wagons loaded with grain, extending from the former Methodist Church, on what is now known as Granville Street, down to the warehouse at the water's edge. This grain was all loaded on outgoing boats. My grandfather went by boat from this landing to Cincinnati in 1864, having volunteered to serve in the army during the Civil War."

John Shepard Johnson was employed, engaged in community life, married, and had children who in his senior years cared for him. One of his sons, James Read Johnson grew up to be a civic leader and benefactor. His grandson, Harry R. Johnson (my grandfather) knew and admired his grandfather.

John's brother George, on the other hand, may have been far more affected by Schuyler's action. According to a letter (November 15, 1949) written by Aunt Mattie: "George ran away from home when he was only twenty-one, and they never heard from him. He was angry at his brother John for telling Uncle Read three months before he was of age that he was going with a circus. Then, when his time was up, he really went. Only once in all those years he heard of him, but not from him."

12. JAMES READ JOHNSON'S
SUCCESSFUL GRAIN BUSINESS

James Read Johnson was born on December 12, 1858, in Baltimore, Fairfield County, Ohio and died on January 6, 1943. He is buried in Old Basil Cemetery, Baltimore, Ohio. James Read Johnson was my great-grandfather.

My mother knew her handsome Grandfather Johnson, a wealthy merchant, town leader and community benefactor. He was the son of John Shepard Johnson and Bell Norris Johnson, the fourth oldest of their ten children. (Four of the ten died as babies or young children.)

James Read Johnson (1858-1943).

James Read Johnson's obituary printed in the *Lancaster Eagle Gazette* on January 7, 1943, states:

> James Read Johnson, 84, one of Baltimore's most prominent citizens, died at 8 p.m. Wednesday in his home as the result of a stroke suffered earlier in the day.
>
> For over 40 years, Mr. Johnson conducted a grain elevator and hay business in Baltimore. He served as president of the First National Bank of Baltimore for a number of years and was a director at the time of his death.
>
> Active in all civic affairs, the deceased donated the land on which Johnson Park recreation center is located. He was a member of the Baltimore Evangelical church.
>
> Survivors include one son, Harry Johnson, Baltimore; seven grandchildren, Sgt. Robert Johnson, Guatemala, Miss Alice Johnson, Washington, D.C., Miss Margaret Johnson, Columbus, Patricia and Marilyn Johnson, all of Baltimore, Mrs. John Hardgrove, Columbus and a great-grandchild, Grace Frances Hardgrove; one sister, Mrs. Ella Alt, Toledo, one brother, Henry Johnson, Butler, Ind., several nieces and nephews.
>
> Rev. L.C. Cooper, Columbus, and Rev. Edward H. Lewis, Baltimore, will officiate at the funeral services to be conducted Saturday at 2 p.m. in the A.E. Johnson Memorial Funeral Home, Baltimore. Burial is to be made in the Basil cemetery.
>
> Friends may call at the Johnson residence after 10 a.m. Friday.

Some clarifying notes to the information provided in the obituary follow.

While James Read (known as J.R.) Johnson's obituary states that he had one surviving son, he had five children. J.R. and his wife Sarah Alice Hansberger Johnson (known as Alice and Allie) had two sons who reached maturity (Arthur E. and Harry R.), two sons who died in infancy and a daughter (Grace) who died at age 16 from an internal goiter. Allie Hansberger Johnson died in 1918 when she fell out of an automobile, broke her hip and was bedfast for a lengthy period. J.R. and Allie had been married for 36 years.

Santa Burton was J.R.'s second wife. They were married in 1920. She had been his housekeeper. They had no children. After Santa's death, J.R. married Lizzie Finefrock, also his housekeeper. Lizzie happened to be Santa's sister. Lizzie had two children from a previous marriage, Louise and Gordon. Louise was the age of Harry R. Johnson's eldest daughter, Alice.

Postcard of J.R. Johnson grain elevator/ mill, Baltimore, Ohio, about 1910.

Mrs. John Hardgrove is J.R.'s brother Arthur's daughter, Nelle Alice Johnson Hardgrove.

My mother's brother, referred to as Sgt. Robert Johnson, was in the U.S. Army in 1943 and was stationed for a time in Guatemala. My mother's sister, Alice Johnson, worked for the federal government in Washington, D.C., in 1943 (during the Second World War). My mother's sister, Margaret Johnson worked as a nurse's aide in Columbus, Ohio. My mother was "Patricia," and her youngest sister was "Marilyn," both schoolgirls living at home.

Mrs. Ella Alt is Aunt Ella, also known as Ellie. Henry Johnson was Aunt Mattie's husband. Ella and Henry were the last of John Shepard Johnson and Bell Norris Johnson's surviving children when J.R. died in 1943.

The obituary is awkward because of the inclusion of "seven grandchildren." J.R.'s surviving son Harry R. Johnson had five children (Alice, Robert, Margaret, Patricia, and Marilyn). The family believed there were only five grandchildren, as the stepchildren of J.R.'s third marriage did not "count."

J.R. Johnson grain elevator/mill building, Baltimore, Ohio, 1978 (photograph by Sandra S. Navarro).

J.R.'s eldest son Arthur was deceased at the time of his father's death. Arthur and his wife Grace had two children. Sadly, Arthur Johnson took his own life in 1935 at the age of 52. Arthur and his family are not mentioned in J.R.'s obituary, except for the confusing inclusion of Mrs. John Hardgrove and Grace Frances Hardgrove. Mrs. John Hardgrove was J.R.'s niece, not his granddaughter, and Grace Frances Hardgrove was J.R.'s grandniece, not his great-grandchild.

Arthur worked in his Uncle Henry Johnson's funeral parlor and furniture business in Baltimore, Ohio. Eventually, Arthur became the owner of this business. He was succeeded in the funeral business by his son Earle who renamed the business the "A.E. Johnson Funeral Home" after his father's death. This is the A.E. Johnson Memorial Funeral Home listed in J.R.'s obituary.

I remember my mother's cousin Earle's funeral home on South Main Street. It was only a few blocks from J.R.'s Victorian-era house where my grandparents lived. Earle Johnson and his wife lived in the funeral home. In my child's eyes, the funeral home looked like just a regular house.

My grandparents' house (referred to in the obituary as "the Johnson residence") was built by my great-grandfather J.R. Johnson and his brothers. My grandfather grew up in this house, and when J.R. died, Grandpa and Grandma moved their family there. This magnificent house on Main Street had front and back staircases, parlor, library, sewing room, kitchen and separate cooking "porch," pantry, and full basement and attic. The grounds of the family home were exciting to me, a youngster who lived in a suburban, mid-century apartment building. There was a barn with nesting mourning doves, grape arbor, "truck patch," and the largest silver maple tree in the entire State of Ohio.

James Read Johnson owned a successful hay and grain business, including a grain mill and elevator, in Baltimore. The artesian well in the area made the development of his grain mill possible. The Johnson grain business was located at North Main Street, Baltimore, Ohio.

The Sanborn Map Company produced a fire insurance map of Baltimore, Ohio in 1895. The map shows "Hansberger Johnson Elevator" (Great-grandma Johnson was Sarah Alice Hansberger Johnson) where the railroad tracks cross Main Street. The building is north of a waterway marked "Ohio Canal." The railroad tracks crossed Main Street south of Front Street.

Today, the site of Great-grandpa Johnson's grain business is on a stretch of Main Street known as North Main Street. The Ohio Canal is gone, and Pawpaw Creek reclaims its rightful place. The railroad tracks are gone. Front Street has been renamed Cliff Street. I saw the building in 1978, but I am uncertain if it now stands, and Google Maps website has not been helpful in answering this question.

In 1918, the *Grain Dealer's Journal* mentions the death of J.R.'s wife, Sarah Alice Hansberger Johnson (referred to as Alice). J.R. is also mentioned in *The Industrial Directory and Shoppers Guide*, 1921.

Among the papers of the Johnson family archive, is a sheet of business letterhead: "Jas. R. Johnson, Buyer and Shipper of Wheat, Corn, Oats and Baled Hay; Dealer in Flour, Feeds, Coal, Wire Fence, Seeds, Etc. Bell Phone 42W, Residence 42N, Baltimore, Fairfield County, Ohio, 193___."

My grandmother's letter to my mother (written April 4, 1957) said that J.R. sold his business to George Daft in 1936 and that Daft sold it to the Farm Bureau Co-op about 1957.

On Labor Day, 1940, Baltimore, Ohio celebrated the dedication of Johnson Park. Grandma saved a souvenir program from this all-day affair.

A "who's who" of Baltimore's citizenry organized the event (approximately 90 people comprising seven committees, falling under the direction of a general chairman). Many of the townspeople's names crop up in my family's letters throughout the years. The dedication was a very big event in this very small town. There was even a Grand Marshall. The program states that in 1935, lifetime resident J.R. Johnson donated a tract of land on South Johnson Street (South Johnson Street is now South Park Street) to the Village of Baltimore, to be used as a City Recreation Park.

In 1936, *The Buckeye Lake News* ran a story about J.R. Johnson. The story describes 78-year-old J.R. Johnson as a community leader unsurpassed in contributing to the development of "the present progressive Baltimore." His 40-year history in the grain business is mentioned as is his 15-year service as president of the First National Bank of Baltimore. His gift of land to the Village of Baltimore is cited as well as his consistent activity with church and civic affairs.

J.R. Johnson left 600 shares of First National Bank stock to each of his son Harry's five children. He left the Victorian home on South Main Street to his son Harry. The "old family silverware" was willed to his granddaughter Alice. Aunt Alice wrote to my mother (February 21, 1979) that she, as J.R.'s first grandchild, had accompanied him everywhere for years.

13. ALONZO ELMER SCHENCK AND IDA RAUCH SCHENCK'S COURTSHIP AND MARRIAGE

Alonzo Elmer Schenck was born on October 28, 1862, in Fairfield County, Ohio and died on March 26, 1954. He is buried in Old Basil Cemetery, Baltimore, Ohio. Alonzo Elmer Schenck was my great-grandfather. Ida Rauch Schenck (named Mary Ida Schenck at birth) was born on September 30, 1864, in Liberty Township, Fairfield County, Ohio and died on May 9, 1939. She is buried in Old Basil Cemetery, Baltimore, Ohio. Ida Rauch Schenck was my great-grandmother.

I remember my great-grandfather from the summer of 1951 when I was about three and a half years old. He lived across the street from my Johnson grandparents (who were his daughter, Ethel Schenck Johnson, and his son-in-law, Harry R. Johnson). He spent time at my grandparents' house, as I did, during that summer.

I called him "Grandpa Schenck." I knew he was Grandma's father. Grandma may have referred to him as "Old Grandpa" to distinguish him from her husband who was, to me, Grandpa Johnson. The name "Old Grandpa" did not stick, though. Everyone called him "Grandpa Schenck."

So, I feel odd when I read documents where he is referred to as "Lon" or "Lonny." "Alonzo" or "A.E." are not so difficult for me, but "Lon" recalls a boy or very young man. In my memory, he is close to 90 years old.

I did not know my great-grandma Ida Rauch Schenck. She died in 1939, prior to my birth. My mother remembered her as a kind person. While I cannot remember my Grandma Johnson talking to me about her mother, the many, many letters they each saved, written to one another over a period of many years, indicate a strong bond between them.

Among the papers saved by my great-grandmother is a handwritten poem. Written at the top of the page is, "This is thy birthday, may it be a source." Also written at the top is, "At home in Ohio, October 28, 1889. To Lonnie."

Alonzo E. Schenck and Ida Rauch Schenck.

The poem has seven stanzas. I suspect that Ida copied it from a source she admired. The fourth stanza is as follows:

> This is thy birthday, may it be
> A source of happiness to thee.
> And may each birthday yet in store
> Be brighter than the one before.

The poem was transcribed on Lon's twenty-seventh birthday.

Lon wrote on the same paper (sending it back to Ida), "Mischief, do you still have to 'float down the stream of life and paddle your own canoe?' If you want a real nice little fellow for a sweetheart, I'll try and find such a one for you. For we have many such among us who would make you an excellent husband and who would not pull their hair when you asked for a new bonnet."

Both Alonzo and Ida grew up on farms in Liberty Township, Fairfield County, Ohio. Both were descendants of Fairfield County pioneers and early settlers. They were both of German heritage and members of the German Reformed Church. They attended camp meetings. They shopped in the same village (Basil, Ohio) and same town (Lancaster, Ohio) and were educated through the eighth grade in public school. I would not be surprised if they had known each other for most of their lives.

Alonzo was a keeper of lists and diaries. Some of these have come to me, including the September page of his 1891 diary. He noted:

September 3. W. Bates, Ida and I went down to Smith's party.

September 4. I went over to Louisa's [Ida's sister's]. Ida came home with me.

September 5. Ida and I went to Lancaster; went out to Wolford's with Will, and I went to singing.

September 6. Went to church in afternoon. Back to Wolford's. Then Will and I went to Christmas Rock, then to Snyder's, then home. Ida and I went to Amanda.

September 7. Ida and I came home by Lancaster.

September 10. Ida Rutherford [Ida's niece] and I went to Basil.

September 13. Nan, Lula, Ida, A. Miller, Ada Schenck, Willie was here today. Wilson Kistler, Ida and I went to Basil.

September 17. Alice [Ida's sister] and I went to Columbus. Alice left for St. Louis at 2:15.

September 20. Took Ida Rutherford home and went to Bethel to a communion. Brought Stella [Ida's niece] home with me in evening.

September 22. Went with Chas. [Ida's brother].

Alonzo E. Schenck, Ida Rauch Schenck, baby Ethel Schenck, 1894.

These entries suggest that Alonzo lived on the Rauch farm before he and Ida were married.

Transcription is tedious going. Alonzo's pencil writing has smeared over the years. His handwriting and spelling are a challenge for me to decipher, and most of the names he mentions are unfamiliar to me. Still, the picture is clear. Alonzo was out and about. He associated with many people in addition to Ida and her relatives. The activities of his church and neighboring churches were important to him.

I believe that Ida's parents objected to courtship. I am able to trace conflict in Rauch family letters. On October 21, 1891, Ida's older sister Alice wrote to her future brother-on-law Alonzo, "It just plucks the heart out of me, the way my people act, but what can I do but let them run their race. I can't see sometimes how Ida can endure it much longer. I glory in your bravery."

One can imagine the upcoming wedding of Ida and Alonzo from this receipt, dated Feb. 18, 1892, from Wm. Stewart (wholesale and retail dealer in Crockery and Glassware, Lamps and Lamp Fixtures), Lancaster, Ohio. For a total of $5.55, Ida and Alzona bought one set of dinner plates, one set of "Han and Teas" [cups?], one butter plate, one bowl, one sauce ladle, two meat dishes, three large nappies, one salt and one pepper duster, one lamp, half dozen engraved tumblers, and one caster.

Alonzo E. Schenck and Ida Rauch Schenck's farm purchased from Silas Gundy, Liberty Township, Fairfield County, Ohio.

Ida and Lon were married on March 6,1892. I have Ida's wedding ring, a simple gold band. It is inscribed, "Ida M. Rauch."

Ida's left these notes in her 1892 almanac, the advertiser from J.A. Kumler's drug store in Baltimore, Ohio: "Married Sunday eve, March 6, '92. Went to Columbus, Monday eve, 7th. Returned Tuesday eve, the 8. Came down to S.W. Blackwoods the 9th eve. Back up home the same eve in the spring wagon and it rained all the way home. Oh, Lord, what a time. Moved the 14th."

"Moved the 14th" suggests that Alonzo lived on the Rauch farm. After their marriage on March 6, they moved to Lithopolis on March 14.

Ida saved a paper in an envelope addressed to "Ida M. Schenck, Lithopolis, Ohio" (postmarked Dumontsville, Ohio, June 5, 1892). On the paper inside, the faded handwriting of Ida's niece, Ida Rutherford (daughter of Ida Rauch Schenck's sister Louise Rauch Rutherford) says:

> Cupid bowed his head to two of the fair youths of Liberty Township on last Sunday evening. The contracting parties being Mr. Alonzo Schenck, a young man of excellent habits, and Ida M. Rauch, a daughter of Mr. John Rauch. She is a lady possessing many admirable traits of character. The marriage was solemnized by Rev. George A. Leonard of Basil in the presence of a few immediate friends after which all partook of an elegant and bountiful supper. Quite a number of handsome and valuable presents were received. They will move upon a farm near Lithopolis where they will endeavor to lead a prosperous and energetic life. May you live long and have a happy life is the wish of best [end of page]"

The paragraph says that they were married in the presence of a few immediate friends. There is no mention of relatives. Surely Ida's sister Alice was at the ceremony? And her brother Roxy? And what of Alonzo's relatives? I know that he was very close to his mother, Sarah Macklin Schenck. This wedding mystery is unsolvable.

Saved receipts reflect the establishment of Ida and Alonzo's household. On March 7, 1892, they purchased from J.M. Bowling ("Dealer in staple and fancy groceries, sugars, spices, canned goods, vegetables, etc., fine teas and coffees a specialty") the following: sugar, rice, soda, tea, hominy, salt, corn, matches, and other goods not legible, for a total of $3.64.

On March 10, 1892, they purchased from J.W. Bowling, lard and oil (total of $4.70).

Three undated receipts from J.M. Bowling, show purchase number one: dish bars, lids, deep pans, wash basin, dipper, sifter, tin cups, large spoon, pot, coffee pot, cook pot, tea kettle, soup pot (total, $4.05).

Schenck farm site, 1978 (photograph taken by Sandra S. Navarro).

Purchase number two is comprised of two skillets, rolling pin, potato masher, clothes basket, clothes line, clothes pins, brush, dunk pan, roaster, basket (total, $8.76). Purchase number three contained two tubs, wash board, coffee mill, baskets, coal hood, oil blinds, hand saw, hatchet, stove pipe, and a few other things that cannot be identified (total, $17.96).

The receipts reflect essential goods and supplies for a farm household in Ohio in 1892.

Alonzo and Ida lived for a year in Lithopolis, Fairfield County, Ohio. They then moved to Marcy, Ohio and lived on a 35-acre farm where my grandmother Ethel was born in 1894 and my great-uncle Noble (Bud) was born in 1897. The family moved to a farm near Marysville, Ohio, in Union County, where my great-aunt Dorothy (Dot) was born in 1902. In 1905, Alonzo and Ida settled on a 50-acre farm "three miles southwest of Basil" which they bought from Silas Gundy (Alonzo's sister Effie's husband).

Three farms, three children, three moves, and so it was that Alonzo and Ida returned to Liberty Township.

14. ETHEL SCHENCK JOHNSON'S SCHOOLS

Ethel Mae Schenck Johnson was born on January 27, 1894, in Marcy, Fairfield County, Ohio and died on July 16, 1968. She is buried in Forest Rose Cemetery, Lancaster, Fairfield County, Ohio. Ethel Mae Schenck Johnson was my grandmother.

Country schoolhouse (remodeled) attended by Ethel Schenck Johnson, Bader Road, Liberty Township, Fairfield County, Ohio (photograph by Sandra S. Navarro, 1978).

As a high school student, I was absorbed by personal narratives about life in the United States. I was fascinated by socio-cultural change and persistence in America. The personal interview was one of my tools to learn about these topics. In September 1965, I interviewed Grandma about her early life. Here is what she told me about going to school.

Ethel Schenck attended a one-room, country school through the eighth grade. The school was heated by a pot-bellied, coal-burning stove. There were double desks for students, a teacher's rostrum and blackboards in front of the classroom. Each class went to the front benches to recite. Her teachers in elementary school were Mr. Sireno West and Miss Pinea Schwartz (whose parents were friends of Ethel's parents). She remembers that boys threw paper wads and wrote notes. She wore a pinafore and high-top laced shoes. Her hair was arranged in a single braid that fell down her back.

Basil High School students, with Ethel Schenck Johnson standing in second row from top, third from left; Basil (now annexed to Baltimore), Ohio.

The Schenck children walked to school or occasionally road in a wagon. In the winter, they rode in a bobsled or sleigh. She repeated the eighth grade because the nearest high school was in Basil, three miles from the farm where she lived. This distance was too far for children to commute. Also, her father thought the eighth grade (the terminal grade for many students) was very important.

Ethel moved to Basil to attend high school in 1909. She lived with Maud Good and Effie Schenck Gundy (her father's sister). This living arrangement did not work out, so Ethel and Eva Paugh drove a horse and buggy to high school from home. Their one-way trip took about three-quarters of an hour. The horse was boarded at Silas Gundy's stable. Ethel fed the horse at midday. Her father met Ethel and Eva in front of the Schencks' farmhouse in the evening to take the horse to the barn. In the winter, Ethel and Eva drove the sleigh. The sleigh was very cold because the seat did not have a back. The girls bundled themselves in robes, heavy coats, gloves, and galoshes.

Basil High School had only about 30 students enrolled in all four grades. The curriculum included instrumental music, and, once a week, a teacher from Columbus provided vocal music. The boys played baseball. There were no formal physical education classes. Ethel studied Latin for four years, English for four years, and algebra, geometry, chemistry, and physics for one year each.

So ended our 1965 interview.

Was Grandma a good student? I did not think to ask her, though I knew she excelled as a writer of well composed, interesting and long letters and that she was an avid reader of books, newspapers and magazines.

Her grade cards provide insight.

Grandma's third grade, year-end report card from the Bonnette School, 1903, provides the following assessment: 98, deportment; 96, studentship; 93, spelling; 96, reading; 95, writing; 93, language; 95, arithmetic; 93, geography.

Grandma's high school freshman, year-end grades from Basil High School, 1910, are: 95, physiology; 91, rhetoric; 91, physical geography; 92, algebra; 94, Latin lessons; 100, deportment.

Grandma's high school senior, year-end grades from Basil High School, 1913, are: 90, psychology; 94, literature; 90, chemistry; 84, geometry; 88, Virgil; 95, music; 100, deportment.

My aunt Alice Johnson Bruce wrote my mother (November 11,1978) about the sightseeing details of my visit to their hometown in 1978. Aunt Alice wrote that we planned to see Grandma's "old home place" on Bader Road and the schoolhouse Grandma attended as a child. The location of the schoolhouse is described as just north of the Schenck farm by about two miles.

Basil High School Class of 1913; Ethel Schenck Johnson standing second from left; Basil (now annexed to Baltimore), Ohio.

Aunt Alice went on to say that she knew the people who live in the little redbrick schoolhouse, converted to a residence: Tom Hall and his wife, "a Paugh girl." My mother, Aunt Alice said, would remember her classmate, Jim Paugh.

Little did Aunt Alice know (or did she?) that nearly seventy years earlier, Grandma commuted to Basil High School with Eva Paugh.

An example of the type of one-room schoolhouse that my grandmother attended is The Poplar Creek School House, preserved by the Baltimore Area Community Museum. It is located on Ohio State Route 256, west of Baltimore, Ohio. Another example of a Liberty Township schoolhouse is the Weakley School, preserved at the Fairfield County Fairgrounds.

My grandmother graduated from Basil High School in 1913. Basil High School was located at 211 North High Street, Basil, Ohio. Basil High School no longer exists. At that location now is Basil Park.

Basil, Ohio no longer exists. It was annexed to Baltimore, Ohio in 1946. Maybe there are still a few people for whom "Basil" has geographic meaning. Maybe there are still a few people who have emotional ties to this nonexistent village.

I may be among those few.

15. THE BALTIMORE HOTEL, VILLAGE ANCHOR

This chapter describes the businesses of the Village of Baltimore, Ohio as they were in the late nineteenth century when The Baltimore Hotel was one of the village anchors. Baltimore was truly a village in the late nineteenth century. Baltimore's population in 1890 was 505, and the population of Basil, the neighboring village, was slightly smaller.

Business Directory of Liberty Township, published in 1875, includes listings from some Baltimore and Basil businesses. A listing was available for a fee, so the business list is not comprehensive. The businesses are as follows: Eli Bishop (Basil carpenter), Michael Friese (Baltimore wagon and carriage manufacturer), V.H. Ginder (Baltimore blacksmith and justice of the peace), Henry Gehring (Baltimore brewer), Anthony Graf (proprietor of Basil Hotel), W.I. Hummel (Baltimore physician and surgeon), J.J. Hausberger [Hansberger] (Baltimore dealer in general merchandise), Chas. Hart (proprietor of Baltimore House), J.H. Harner (Basil dealer in general merchandise), T.J. Kirk (Baltimore painter), John Laver (Basil foundryman), Peter Macklin (Basil carpenter), Neff Miller (Baltimore brick and tile manufacturer), Daniel Roly [Roley] (Basil carpenter), Samuel Rader (Baltimore ship carpenter), J.P.H. Stephenson (Basil physician and surgeon), R.C. Soliday [Saliday] (Baltimore wagon maker), J.D. Stith (Basil wood trader), John Smeck (Baltimore miller and dealer in grain and coal), John W. Whitely (Baltimore ship carpenter), Jacob Wildermuth (Baltimore proprietor of sawmill), G.W. Watson (Baltimore druggist), and W.F. Wayne (Basil physician and surgeon).

Baltimore Hotel building, Baltimore, Ohio, 1978
(photograph taken by Sandra S. Navarro).

The directory also includes teachers, ministers and many, many farmers.

The Sanborn Map Company produced a fire insurance map of Baltimore, Ohio in 1895. Baltimore businesses are labeled on this map: two blacksmiths, railroad and freight depot, Hansberger and Johnson elevator, Wildermuth lumber company, Buckeye planning mill, grist mill, bakery and restaurant, tailor, three general stores, Baltimore Hotel and dining room, cigar store, drugs and paints, meat store, restaurant, general store, two harness shops, jewelry store, cobbler, three doctors' offices, carpenter, two "lodge rooms," hardware and furniture store, drugstore, combined post office and general store, newspaper printing office, and H.E. Smart paper mill.

I recognize my relatives' businesses in the above list: J.J. Hansberger's general store, Peter Macklin's carpentry business, and Hansberger and Johnson's grain elevator. Among the individuals named as having businesses in Baltimore and Basil are other distant relatives and relatives by marriage, and townspeople long associated with generations of my ancestors.

The Baltimore Hotel is named. The Sanborn insurance map shows the Baltimore Hotel at corner of Main and Canal Streets. Main Street is Ohio State Route 158, and Canal Street has been renamed Cliff Street. (This Baltimore Hotel is not the same as the Hotel Baltimore (1874-1923) located at 539 South Main Street.)

There were six hotels in Baltimore, Ohio between 1886 and 1915, during the so-called "Oil Boom" of Baltimore's history.

Great-grandpa Alonzo E. Schenck bought the Baltimore Hotel in 1920 from his cousin William L. Buchanan. Past purchases of the hotel property are confusing. The deeds that Grandpa Schenck saved (and were then saved by Grandma, then by my mother) document the transfers of ownership.

Postcard of Main Street, looking south, Baltimore, Ohio, about 1910.

Here's the complicated string of events: Elizabeth Jan Wildermuth and Jacob Wildermuth sold the properties known as the Baltimore Hotel and hotel barn to William L. Buchanan in 1894. In 1896, the "inlot" was sold by George and Katie Miller to William L. Buchanan. Also in 1896, William Whitecamp and Mary Whitecamp sold "inlots" to William L. Buchanan. In 1905, William and Cassie Buchanan sold a hotel property to William H. Leitnaker. In 1909, William L. Buchanan and Cassie Buchanan sold a hotel property to Rebecca Loose.

By the way, the mother of my great-grandmother Sarah Alice Hansberger Johnson was Elizabeth Loose Hansberger.

Finally, in 1920, William L. Buchanan sold the Baltimore House (west of the hotel) and livery barn to Alonzo Schenck.

The tale is complicated. I was told that Alonzo and Ida Schenck owned the Baltimore Hotel, but the last deed refers to the structure as the "Baltimore House." They owned the property from 1920 until 1926. The address is certain: 217 North Main Street, Baltimore, Ohio. In 1978, my Aunt Alice showed me the two-story brick building.

From the vantage point of Google Maps, the structure appears to now be an apartment building.

Blacksmithies, wagon-making establishments and harness stores have come and gone, but the "Baltimore Hotel" (or "Baltimore House") is standing still at 217 North Main Street, Baltimore, Ohio. It continues to anchor the village.

16. PIONEERS TO DESCENDANTS

This book contains fifteen stories about people in Fairfield County, Ohio: pioneers, early settlers and their nineteenth-century descendants. The stories take place in Liberty Township and Baltimore and Basil, Ohio.

These narratives about people in nineteenth-century Ohio have passed through generations. They spotlight family strife, personal tragedy and social values such as caring for children, providing for ailing family members, and, occasionally, seeking individual opportunity and fulfillment.

Many details of these stories were hidden in family archives and public records, but the bare bones of these stories lived in family lore far beyond the time when the events took place. I have long known about Great-great-great-grandpa Peter Macklin's meerschaum pipes, Great-great-great-grandma Nancy Read's tabletop tombstone and the enduring Baltimore Hotel, for instance.

When I visited Baltimore, Ohio (and by extension Basil, Ohio) in the 1950s and 1960s, I was known by many villagers. I was repeatedly recognized even though I had lived there for only a few months as an infant and for brief periods of vacation from school.

As an adult, I understand that the villagers were not simply recognizing a visiting child. Rather, they were acknowledging and validating shared historical, social and cultural connections. The villagers were right about these connections. I, a twentieth and twenty-first-century descendant and by many measures an outsider, carry a sense of belonging to pioneers and early settlers of Liberty Township, Baltimore and Basil, Ohio.

OTHER BOOKS IN THE CORNSILK PRESS
FAMILY STORYTELLER SERIES

Cooking with My Ancestors

Oslo to Ohio: Erika's Story, 1899-1955

Ethel's Archives: A Family History from Baltimore, Ohio

*Chickering Read's Grave and Other Tales
from 400 Years of an American Family*

See www.cornsilkpress.com for more information.

www.ingramcontent.com/pod-product-compliance
Lightning Source LLC
Chambersburg PA
CBHW060547100426
42742CB00013B/2482